Entrepreneur.
VOICES

ON

CAREERS

D0558785

The Staff of Entrepreneur Media, Inc.

Entrepreneur Press®

Entrepreneur Press, Publisher
Cover Design: Andrew Welyczko
Production and Composition: Eliot House Productions

This publication is designed to provide accurate and
authoritative information in regard to the subject matter covered.
It is sold with the understanding that the publisher is not
engaged in rendering legal, accounting or other professional
services. If legal advice or other expert assistance is required, the
services of a competent professional person should be sought.

Entrepreneur Press® is a registered trademark of Entrepreneur
Media, Inc.

Library of Congress Catalog-in-Publishing Data has been
    applied for.
LC record available at https://lccn.loc.gov/2019025962
ISBN-13: 978-1-59918-659-7

Printed in the United States of America
23 22 21 20   10 9 8 7 6 5 4 3 2 1

CONTENTS

PART II
PRO TIPS FOR SIDE GIGS

Contents

FOREWORD BY DEBBIE ALLEN

Motivational business speaker and author of Success is Easy: Shameless No-Nonsense Strategies to Win in Business

Success requires you to listen to your own voice. No one can define success for you. You must discover and define success on your own terms. To do that, you may need to travel down a few career paths before you arrive at the place that feels just right for you.

You'll know once you've arrived at your destination because it begins to tap into your true, authentic core being. A successful career can often feel like your special gift, or what you've been put on this earth to do. We all seek to find that career that speaks to us in this way.

Some of us are lucky enough to experience that special career once or more in life, but only if we pay attention, listen carefully, and are open to new horizons. You must be willing to ask for what you most desire, and never settle for less that you deserve.

Getting a big paycheck doesn't necessarily define true success. I know plenty of people who would define their careers as "wearing the golden handcuffs." They stay for the nice corporate paycheck and company benefits, yet feel bound by an unsatisfying career. They count the months or years until they can leave their corporate jobs as if they were talking about serving time.

Well, that's actually what they're doing: serving time until they can take off the "golden handcuffs" to begin a new career and a new life that's more fulfilling and more authentically true to what they desire.

As they sit and wait out their time, they often dream of a new career direction that will excite and challenge them much more than their current position. They often dream of leaving their corporate job and starting their own company and doing things on their own terms, on their own time, in their own way.

Some of them have a very specific business idea in mind they want to start, while others seek out a franchise company they believe in with an established brand and systemized process already in place to invest in. No matter what path they choose, the one thing they know for sure is that the voice inside of their head is speaking to them loud and clear, telling them they are ready to move on.

I know the feeling of being bound in a career, even inside of my own business. I've outgrown my own entrepreneurial career many times due to feeling unchallenged, bored, or just knowing it was time for a change or reinvention. My motto in business is, "If it's not fun, I'm not doing it anymore!"

When this feeling comes over me, I know I'm ready for a change or another big reinvention. I've reinvented myself so many times in business you could call me the Queen of Reinvention.

In business, you can't be afraid of tackling change and reinventing yourself. That's how you advance, move ahead, and truly succeed. To do this, you'll need to tap into your intuition and know when it's guiding you to make a change. Ignoring it will not serve you. In fact, change may even be forced upon you. If you are going to make a change, you want to make sure it's your own choice—not someone else's choice.

Foreword by Debbie Allen

Maybe you don't know what that change or transition looks like just yet. Don't worry, that's okay. With awareness, you'll begin to see new opportunities placed in front of you, almost like magic. Those opportunities were there all along—you just didn't notice or pay attention to them until now.

It's possible that you are feeling bored, unappreciated, or undervalued in your current career. Or, maybe you are in need of an advancement to feel more challenged or to expand your skills. And, you may want to reinvent yourself completely to tackle a new entrepreneurial business venture that you've been passionate about for a long time. So, how do you know when you are ready for a career change, transition, or complete reinvention?

You listen. You listen to yourself. You're here right now because you've probably already heard that voice inside of your head, or tapped into your intuition that's guiding you towards change. Pay attention to that voice inside you that says, "It's time for a change. It's time to start a new journey."

To help guide you along your journey are 25 career experts in this book that openly share their career insights. They address phases and transitions of all kinds from inside the corporate culture to building multimillion-dollar entrepreneurial business ventures. Allow their personal stories to inspire your own positive voice of transition and change for growth and success. You already know you want to go somewhere new. Let these writers help show you the way.

FORGE YOUR OWN CAREER PATH

The corporate world has taken us down a very long, winding road from Cubeville to "crushing it" culture. Along the way, we went from a generation of 30-plus year corporate vets with retirement watches on our wrists to a new world of side hustlers and serial entrepreneurs. In other words, the world of work—specifically, the career landscape—has changed.

Now, the word "career" contains multitudes. More than just a job that you leave at the end of the day, your career dovetails with several areas of your life—home, relationships, family, lifestyle, social footprint, and even personal worldview. This is not to say that a career should be the driving force in your life or that workaholism is a sustainable practice. But rather, that our lives are intricate tapestries with our careers serving as a connective thread. Our lifestyles inform our career choices, and vice versa.

Taking stock of who you are and what you want out of a career isn't a task you can (or should) complete in one sitting. Because your career evolves as your lifestyle does, your needs and priorities shift in kind. What that means on a cellular level is that you are constantly assessing and evaluating your career, making tweaks as you advance along your path.

For some people, that amounts to changing jobs on the regular. According to the U.S. Bureau of Labor Statistics, the average person will change jobs 12 times in their career, staying at each job roughly four years. That number changes with age, however, with younger workers (25 to 34) holding shorter-tenured jobs for an average of 2.8 years, and older workers (45 to 54) for 7.6 years. Mid-Millennials (35 to 44) stick around in the four-year range, while those near retirement (age 55 and up) hang in for around 10 years. No matter your age, changing jobs is likely a move you will make at some point.

However, the impetus to make that move and rethink your career path looks different for each of us. So, choose your own adventure. Maybe you want to move up the ranks within your existing company. This is the path of the intrapreneur, someone who uses the best practices of entrepreneurship in their company to innovate and build personal brand awareness. Or, perhaps you see a path adjacent to your current career that you want to pursue while still pulling in a regular paycheck. You, friend, are a side hustler. Been there, done that? If so, it may be time to fly and take that big leap into the entrepreneurial unknown.

The editors of Entrepreneur have got you covered for any of these scenarios in *Entrepreneur Voices on Careers*. We've assembled an all-star team of entrepreneurs who have their eyes on the career horizon and can walk you through the intricacies of how to enhance and advance your career. This book lays out the key ingredients to creating an effective career plan. It takes a deep dive into how to build your personal work brand, navigate the complexities of corporate life, make the moves you need to advance your career to the next level, create viable options for your move into entrepreneurship, and ultimately create an exit strategy that sets you up for long-term success. There is truly no better time to create a new career plan, and this book will help you get started. Let's go!

ADVICE FOR THE INTRAPRENEUR

Everyone is an intrapreneur these days. Whether you work for a multinational, Fortune 500 behemoth or a small, family-owned business on Main Street, you have the ability to make your mark on the company. One way you can do that is to be an intrapreneur—someone who makes smart entrepreneurial moves within a company to help it grow in new directions and also to expand your own career.

And since we live in a golden age of personal branding, everyone is building their brand, whether online or in person. That's an idea not lost on cube dwellers—especially ones who want to be recognized as innovators within their industries. By using smart entrepreneurial moves within the company you work for, you can brand yourself as an agent of positive change who not only drives their own work forward, but that of their colleagues and company as well.

The beauty of intrapreneurship is that you don't have to go it alone. You can grow that personal brand and entrepreneurial skill set with a safety net—the one your company provides. For example, have you ever wanted to try a new method for project management but knew you couldn't jump ship and start your own management firm? Why not test drive your theories at your current company, where you can get the support you need and help promote stronger employee engagement for your boss? Do you see a challenge in product development that you want to solve? Pitch that solution to the team you work with now, and work out the kinks in corporate before you set out on your own. The intrapreneurial possibilities are endless.

All that said, being an intrapreneur is not necessarily a means to an end. Yes, many intrapreneurs have one foot out the door.

But there are just as many who have found a home in corporate and want to grow and thrive there for the long haul. They see a path that leads to strong career growth, so they use their inner intrapreneur to help them rise up the ladder right to the C-Suite.

In this section, you'll find information and insight for all kinds of intrapreneurs. Whether you're a side hustler or a ladder climber, we've got you covered. From taking stock of your career journey to finding new and useful ways to be your own boss (even if you work for someone else), these chapters will walk you through the experience of the intrapreneur and hopefully inspire you to start building your own personal work brand.

NOT YOUR PARENTS' CAREER DEVELOPMENT

Isa Watson

For my parents, a career meant one thing: progressing through the ranks at a single company and climbing a corporate ladder where growth could be measured through regular raises and promotions.

But today, progress in a career is rarely linear. The average millennial changes jobs four times in the first decade out of college—more than double the previous generation. And many employers expect their employees to stay for less than two years. In this environment of constant change, it's not surprising that the meaning behind a career has started to shift—and not just in one direction. These changes have introduced a multiplicity. There's now an unprecedented variety in the shapes a career can take.

My own career has evolved across industries. I started out as a diabetes chemist and data scientist at Pfizer. After earning my MBA, I shifted into finance, joining a rotational leadership program and becoming the vice president of digital product and strategy at JPMorgan Chase. Then, I started my own company, Envested. Determined to change how people connect at work, I was able to create connections across my diverse skill set and broad network to build innovative solutions. My path hasn't been linear, but I've been able to chart a course from science to finance to tech, with each step increasing my capacity to learn.

A Wider View of Success

This shift in the idea of what a career can be has also impacted our definition of success. If you can't track progress in the same way, it only makes sense that there would be uncertainty surrounding whether you have "made it." Need proof? Just look at the lists of podcasts trying to unravel what success and fulfillment mean today. And it makes sense. If you aren't moving up a ladder or following an established path, how do you know how much progress you've made?

That's not to say that the typical symbols of success like wealth and titles, don't matter—they still do—but people now think about the idea in broader, more encompassing terms. Today, success can mean getting to do the thing you're most passionate about or creating a positive change in the world. It can mean pushing your talents to their limits or being able to adapt to whatever is thrown your way. Success can also mean building the talents of those around you, and it can mean being able to look back without any regrets.

Own Your Career Strategy

Of course, when success can mean so many things, it's up to you as an individual to choose which aspects matter most. But even having set a vision, it can be hard to see which path represents the best way to achieve it. Our parents might have managed their careers in reaction to company shifts or personal changes, but today, it's necessary to be proactive in setting a direction, especially when, according to a 2017 survey by Willis Towers Watson, less than half of employees believe their employers provide useful career-planning tools or opportunities to advance their careers.

So how do you keep yourself on the path to continual growth, no matter the direction? You don't need to wait for a big opportunity or life-changing moment. To be proactive in your career, focus on these three things every week.

Meet Someone New

People talk a lot about the importance of having a strong network when looking to change roles, but the benefits of professional connections go far beyond job-switching. Your growth is limited if it's happening in a silo. Instead, meeting new people—whether they're peers, potential mentors, or experts in areas you want to learn more about—will increase your exposure to new perspectives and provide insight into your own development. You don't need to have coffee dates lined up every day of the week, but reaching out to just one or two new contacts a week is a great way to manageably meet new people and practice your soft skills. Even better, it's also an opportunity to meet a potential new friend.

Take Stock of What You've Learned

All accomplishments are built on a foundation of what you've learned. So no matter how you envision your success, you should be keeping track of how you've grown on a weekly and monthly basis, including both formal and informal learning opportunities. Knowing exactly what skills you've added to your wheelhouse or how your perspective has expanded will also put you in a stronger position when raising your hand to take on expanded responsibilities or putting your hat in the ring for a promotion or leadership role. Reflecting on what you've learned is also a great opportunity to celebrate any wins. While it's often easy to focus on what's still left to be done, being your own cheerleader is crucial to maintaining motivation.

Set a New Goal

After you look back to see what you've learned, it's equally important to set your sights on future progress by specifying one thing you want to accomplish in the upcoming week. This can be something you want to learn or one task to cross off your list. Whatever it is, it should be something that stretches you but is also manageable and realistic. For example, if you want to learn a new skill, set a goal one week to research online tutorials; the next week, vow to spend 30 minutes per day on your selected course. If you want to start volunteering to use your skills in a new environment, you can set a goal of researching nonprofits one week and then reaching out to a certain number each day thereafter. Like any good goal, your weekly career goal should be clear and measurable and, to build momentum, should naturally lead into the next goal on your list.

While career development today is very different from what our parents experienced, owning your career and finding opportunities for continued growth will set the stage for continued success—no matter what path your career takes.

2

THREE UNWRITTEN RULES WOMEN NEED TO KNOW FROM THE CORPORATE WORLD

Sharon E. Jones

Do you know what you need to do to succeed at your company? One major challenge is that beyond your defined job responsibilities there are unwritten rules of corporate culture that aren't covered in any orientation or employee handbook. These unwritten rules were formed decades ago when the workplace was predominantly male.

Unwritten behavioral norms that arose in workplace cultures dominated by men may seem foreign to women due to differences in upbringing. Many women are raised not to call attention to their own accomplishments or intelligence. Furthermore, many women are socialized to believe that taking center stage is unladylike and improper. Many men do not receive the same messaging. This difference in messaging ends up putting women at a disadvantage as they navigate their careers.

Far too often, hardworking, intelligent women get passed over for promotions and overlooked for high-profile work assignments and just don't know why. One reason this happens is because women often don't know how to navigate the unwritten rules of corporate culture.

To help level the playing field for women, here are three foundational, unwritten rules of the corporate world. If you want to advance into leadership at your company, ask yourself if you have been investing time and resources into each of these areas.

Recruit a Sponsor

Both mentors and sponsors give advice, provide feedback and make introductions to people in their networks. The key difference is that sponsors are people who are in "the room where it happens," to reference the *Hamilton* song. Sponsors are people who have power and influence and are willing to use their position to advocate on your behalf.

When the Center for Talent Innovation (CTI) asked professionals if they had a sponsor, only 13 percent of female professionals and just 8 percent of professionals of color reported having a sponsor, compared to 40 percent of their non-diverse peers. Lack of sponsorship is likely one of the reasons why there are so few diverse leaders in the corporate world. Read Sylvia Ann Hewlett's book *Forget a Mentor, Find a Sponsor* to get a clearer sense of what good sponsors do. Remember that if an individual either a) lacks the necessary power and influence or b) is not willing to advocate on your behalf, then he or she is not your sponsor.

Relationships with sponsors do not just go one way—ensure you are an excellent protégé and give back to your sponsors when the opportunities arise. Also, don't conflate sponsors and mentors. They are each important to career success but different in role and function. Mentors can be at your level or higher than you. Sponsors by definition are higher because they are in a position of power and influence. Mentors can help guide you and provide informal feedback and information. Sponsors need to be willing to put their "chips" on you, but they don't have time for every question you may have. That is what your mentor is for.

Strategically Self-Promote

In the corporate world, it is expected that you will highlight your accomplishments. If you don't, your unspoken accomplishments will be overshadowed by the accomplishments of your office mates who ensure their good news is circulated through the office chatter.

The default perception is that a worker is average or below average, unless demonstrated otherwise. If people start off with a neutral or negative perception of your ability, it is your responsibility to present them with positive facts about yourself, so they can form a more accurate, positive perception of you. This is particularly important if you are a diverse professional, because you will likely have to push back against negative stereotypes often associated with your identity.

Effective self-promotion is about being proud of what you worked hard to accomplish and willingly sharing those stories with others. For self-promotion strategies on how to develop your story and deliver it with conviction, read *BRAG! The Art of Tooting Your Own Horn without Blowing It* by Peggy Klaus.

Invest in Your Professional Appearance

Before we even open our mouths, we make an impression just by how we present ourselves. Your colleagues may judge your level of professionalism and bucket you into a particular social class by the way you dress. If you are a diverse professional, the way you dress may support or contradict the unconscious stereotypes that people may carry in their heads. Therefore, be mindful about managing your image and consider how it will be viewed by others.

One of the best examples of image management is Beyoncé. You rarely find an ugly image of Beyoncé on social media or even in print. Reportedly, Beyoncé spends $1 million per year on hair, makeup and other self-care. You don't need to spend $1 million, but when presenting yourself, make sure others see you the way you want to be seen.

As a guide on how to dress, look to the people in leadership positions at your organization. There may be some quirky leaders at your office with a unique sense of style but defer to the majority of your senior colleagues. Emulate the level of professional appearance of your organization's leaders to the extent that your budget will allow. Looking the part is an important component of rising through the ranks.

Pay Attention to What Matters

Continue to work hard each and every day, but also focus on some of the other areas that matter: recruiting sponsors, strategically self-promoting your work, and investing in your professional appearance. With insider knowledge of some areas that often get overlooked, you can be more strategic and less reactive in your career.

ENTREPRENEUR VOICES SPOTLIGHT: INTERVIEW WITH BENJAMIN GILAD AND MARK CHUSSIL

Benjamin Gilad and Mark Chussil are authors of *The New Employee Manual: A No-Holds-Barred Look at Corporate Life* (Entrepreneur Press, 2019). Gilad is a former strategy professor at Rutgers University and a current war gaming trainer for the Fortune 500. He is the president of two companies, www.giladwargames.com and www.academyci.com, but not the boss at home (where his wife and kids rule). The rest is uninteresting, pompous hype, and too corporate to list here. Chussil is the founder of Advanced Competitive Strategies, Inc., an adjunct instructor at the University of Portland, and a four-decade veteran of competitive strategy. He is the author of *Strategy Analysis with ValueWar* and *Nice Start*, and has contributed content for five other books and numerous articles for Entrepreneur, the *Harvard Business Review*, and elsewhere.

Entrepreneur: How did you get into the world of war games? What is your origin story?

Gilad: It was such a long time ago. I truly don't remember. All I know is that I was hunting mammoths with my clan, and at some point I said, "We need to consider the mammoths' perspectives, intentions, and capabilities if we want to avoid surprises." You see, one of the mammoths turned around and stepped on my cousin, flattening him significantly. Oh, and yes, the Kellogg Company asked me to create a competitive intelligence system for it in the 80s and as the first assignment we ran a war game for Corn Flakes. To date, I don't eat Cheerios (non-Kellogg's cereal).

Chussil: I planned to become a professor of political science. I would wear tweed jackets with suede elbow patches and adoring students would cherish every word I said. Did you know that "utopia" melds "eutopia" (the good place) and "outopia" (no place)? I accidentally got an MBA instead. Computers looked like fun, so with the help of several extraordinary people, I learned how to write competitive-strategy simulators. My former business partner got us a project simulating strategy alternatives for a major chemicals company. I didn't even know we were conducting a business war game.

Gilad: Mark's story explains why I don't believe in long term planning.

Chussil: Ben's story explains why I don't believe in Cheerios.

Entrepreneur: What are some of the challenges for people who are trying to thrive and survive in the corporate world? What advice would you give to overcome/address those challenges?

Gilad: Corporate provides security and health insurance and in return asks for complete and utter conformity to the internal narrative—even when it is competitively bonkers. So if you are strategically inclined, you are watching an inevitable decline and can't do anything about it. One way to overcome it is to become the CEO by schmoozing. Another is to catch the attention of the CEO with intriguing alternative narrative, which means you need to develop one, which is not easy if all you want is to do your job and go home. Yet another is to get out fast. My personal favorite is to always—*always*—try to find the boss that likes *iconoclastic* views.

Chussil: I survived but didn't thrive even in "small-c" corporate. I care about creativity, discovery, and the quality of decisions, and although those things certainly matter, they're not the heart of everyday corporate life. So, my first bit of advice is to face your reality. Figure out what kind of job fits you. Second bit of advice: You will change during your life, so remember that what fits you will also change during your life. A third bit: Be honest with yourself. There are always tradeoffs on any path you choose. Finally: Don't spend your life making up your mind. If you do want a corporate job, ask lots of sincere questions, especially of people higher up the hierarchy. Show you want to learn. Use what you learn.

Gilad: Mark is a good person who believes in being honest with oneself. If I am honest with myself, I get a headache.

Chussil: "The most important thing in acting is honesty; once you learn to fake that, you're in," so says Samuel Goldwyn.

Entrepreneur: What are some of the best ways people can honor their inner maverick while staying within the confines of capital-C Corporate? What do those options look like?

Gilad: Find people like you. Form a support group and call it a Competitive Think Tank. Whisper, "They are blind!" in the broom closet when no one around; overtly, in meetings, always try and inject the perspective of *other* market players. Ask, "Can we look at it from their perspective for just one second? Where is their weak link we can use to our advantage by things *differently*?"

Chussil: Warning: I love teaching and public speaking, but I'm an introvert. If you're an extravert, you might want to listen to—excuse me—talk with someone else. If you want to stay with your company, then Ben's advice about the Competitive Think Tank, is spot on. If you plan to change companies, go into consulting, or launch your own business, practice thinking like a scientist. Observe the people and decision-making around you now. Notice not only *what* they decide but also *how* they decide. Ask yourself over and over: why would a *smart* person do what they're doing? You don't have to agree with them, but you will see the corporate world differently, and seeing the world differently is your first step to doing something differently.

Gilad: Mark and I agree that understanding the *why* behind action explains a lot about people, companies, and even politicians. Well, OK, maybe not politicians. Mark did say "smart person." And did you note he wrote *extra*vert, not extrovert? He is that precise. He tried to make me precise, too. I gave him a headache.

Chussil: I know it's impolite to return a gift, but I gave the headache back to Ben. Often.

Entrepreneur: A lot of people find that once they start a new job, it doesn't quite match the job description they were hired to do. What's a maverick to do when that happens?

Gilad: Grieve, lose weight, get depressed, or understand life is not fair and make lemonade out of the health benefits. Face it, newbie: If you believed the job description to begin with, you shouldn't be asking why reality is different. Ask instead, "How can I be as cynical as Ben? As smart as Mark?"

Chussil: You can be an optimist, but optimists are never pleasantly surprised. You can be a pessimist, but pessimists don't have much fun. I guess you're in trouble either way.

Gilad: Think of job descriptions as food commercials. They are never as good as they look.

Chussil: We talk about food commercials in our book! A single-serving cereal box promised 100 percent* of the daily requirements of some vitamins and minerals. Did you notice the asterisk in the previous sentence? If you could find the footnote, you'd see that a 53g portion of the cereal indeed provides that wonderful nutrition, but the box contained only 33g of the cereal. Job descriptions can be like that, so be careful. You are what you eat.

Entrepreneur: The word "competitive" often gets a bad rap when it comes to workplace culture, but you advocate for having a competitive mindset in the workplace. Walk us through your outlook on competition.

Gilad: There are corporate cultures pitting teams against each other inside the same company. There are cultures hailing collaboration above all. Both can produce good results or bad results. There are fads and slogans, but no one model that works best. But the iron rule should be that competing internally never rises to a level of forgetting to compete externally, which supersedes everything else for the simple reason that if you compete harder internally than externally you'd be competing to get to the unemployment line first.

Chussil: Ben and I argued often as we wrote our book, but we were not competitive. We weren't trying to beat each other. We were trying to understand, learn, and get smarter together. We were practicing the mindset and skill of *competing*. We helped our best thinking rise to the top so our book would succeed in the marketplace. Notice, too, that merely being "competitive" could mean writing clickbait, empty slogans, and even nonsense. We wanted to compete with a superior-quality product.

Ben and I both conduct business war games, and "war game" sure sounds competitive. War is a zero-sum game where one side must lose for the other to win. But there is nothing in business strategy that *requires* zero-sum thinking. Market share is a zero-sum game because there is always, always exactly 100-percent market share to go around. But profit, customer satisfaction, employee satisfaction, corporate responsibility, etc., are not zero-sum games. Competing well doesn't mean crushing the competition. It means being smart.

Gilad: Indeed, "war game" is a total misnomer. Business is not war and for many making money is not a game, but it beats the alternative name of "You didn't think about that, did you?" (YDTATDY).

Chussil: Well said. I tried "strategy game" and "virtual competition," and they bombed. I'm inclined to blame the customer (heresy!) for the terminology. Still, as terminology goes, it's not as bad as "certified pre-owned."

3

DRIVE INNOVATION BY REDISCOVERING YOUR INTRINSIC ENTREPRENEURIAL MINDSET

Angela Kambouris

Developing an entrepreneurial mindset doesn't require an MBA or millions of dollars. It does, however, demand that you're willing to imagine new ways to solve problems, embrace failure, and create extraordinary value.

Most people associate entrepreneurship with the stuff of fairy tales. The most successful among them have become near-archetypes—the rags-to-riches underdog (Howard Schultz), the unorthodox and unapologetic visionary (Steve Jobs), the adventurer (Richard Branson). Now all are famous, maybe even "heroic" by modern standards. They captured headlines along with our imaginations and accumulated staggering wealth.

Despite their unique imprints, though, these archetypes show that one thing remains true: The entrepreneurial mind is something you can attain, with knowledge learned through experience and exploration.

Those who possess the entrepreneurial spirit are motivated by love of their product or service. They have an innate passion for making a difference in the world. Many don't actually want to strike out alone— at least, not initially. They want to add value within their organizations, improve their ability to chart new paths, or challenge the status quo to become a force for innovation. At some point, though, they experience a shift in mindset. They recognize they can explore and amplify their inherent drives.

Entrepreneurial thinking powers industries, transforming companies from within and creating extraordinary value for employees and customers. Much like artists or composers, entrepreneurs see something no one else sees. Then they surround themselves with other talented performers to bring that vision to life.

Promoting an entrepreneurial mindset company-wide can help you gain a competitive edge and create opportunities for growth. It can be a means to improve products, processes and services; to acquire and retain new clients; and to attract and retain quality people in the business.

Here's how to get started.

Live the Values Every Day

Entrepreneurs are driven by purpose. Within the corporate arena, people often act within the confinements of their roles. When you integrate entrepreneurial thinking into the walls of an organization, you give people a reason to get out of bed. Connecting their hearts and minds to a shared vision gives more context to each role. Help your team members find their inner purpose and imbue meaning in what they do, regardless of their title or seniority within the organization.

Keep It All About the Client

Organizations that obsess over customers are acutely tuned in to their wants and needs. A client-centric approach is about delivering high-quality products or services while creating real relationships to drive repeat business, loyalty, and profits. When employees act like entrepreneurs, the center of focus shifts to the clients.

When you shift that focus to clients or customers, you can open doors to new conversations that help drive your business. So, encourage your team to ask open-ended questions that lead to quality conversations:

- What does the customer want, need, or desire?
- What are the customer's pain points and frustrations?
- How can each team member improve interactions with clients to serve them better, faster, or with less drama?

These questions tap into the essence of the client experience. The answers paint a valuable picture of what's important and how your product or service adds value. If challenges arise, these exercises also position you to offer real solutions.

Seek Out Incubator Experiences

Empowering people to explore new, better ideas and processes can foster forward thinking, bring about positive changes, and create room for innovation. These typically are semi-protected spaces where people can share and debate ideas, then mold them into new forms. These spaces might be an internal committee, a secret Facebook group, or an incubator experience or roundtable.

Leave the Ego at the Door

Ever met a human who hasn't made a mistake? Organizations are renowned for blaming and shaming people when errors go public. Instead, use mistakes as an opportunity for everyone to learn. Promoting entrepreneurial thinking means supporting people to leave their ego to the side. Challenge them to think of themselves as CEOs of their world, instilling a culture of responsibility, ownership, and accountability for their results.

Find the Sweet Spot

Entrepreneurial organizations have a culture of working hard and playing hard. Leaders place high expectations on their people, adopt a no-room-for-mediocrity attitude, and have a high regard for a strong work ethic. Find the sweet spot: Ensuring your company is fun also can be vital to its success.

Take Advantage of Teachable Moments

Entrepreneurial champions are worth their weight in gold. Instill an attitude of mentoring to communicate that you are here to help people unlock their potential, facilitate coaching moments, and close the gap to achieve the results they want. Lead people and coach in real time. Doing so will help you inspire your workforce to be part of the collective success.

Embrace a Greater Social Responsibility

Entrepreneurial thinkers create a space to be more agile, innovative, and resilient. They share a commitment to conducting business responsibly and showing respect for people, communities, and the environment. Companies with a genuine desire to make a sustainable difference instill these values throughout their organization. For example, Unilever made numerous changes in factories around the world to create more sustainable, environmentally friendly operations. The company implemented a Sustainable Living Plan to increase positive social impact and support the UN Sustainable Developmental Goals.

Cultivate a Culture of Intimacy

Entrepreneurial organizations deliberately maintain a strong sense of connection with both their people and their customers. This togetherness is an investment in providing all employees with opportunities for real business involvement, including decision-making and innovations. Such companies capitalize on individual strengths and connect individuals inside and outside the organization to work on projects.

Client engagement is more a sense of partnership where regular events, product testing, and feedback provide insight and excitement about products and loyalty to the brand.

Become a Perpetual Learner

Most of us have forgotten how to tap into our natural, entrepreneurial spirit. Enrolling in a course is one way to reignite our curiosity. Many universities dedicate centers to teaching entrepreneurial skills. If there isn't an actual campus in your area, opt for the virtual version: Udemy, Coursera, or Skillshare are a few to consider.

Discover Clues to Success in Others' Stories

You don't need a one-on-on audience to learn from some of the world's most successful entrepreneurs. If you want to test the road less traveled, *Tribe of Mentors* tackles a wide range of topics. Tim Ferriss offers his own advice and pulls insights from influential mentors. Gary Vaynerchuk shares his experience and offers strategies, tactics, and inspiration from others in *Crushing It!: How Great Entrepreneurs Build Their Business and Influence—and How You Can, Too.*

I'M THE CEO OF A MULTIMILLION-DOLLAR COMPANY WITHOUT GOING TO COLLEGE

Suresh Sambandam

Look at a list of successful entrepreneurs, and it's pretty easy to spot the demographic patterns. Most of those who are household names are white, well-connected males from the upper strata of society with access to capital and degrees from famous colleges.

But that doesn't have to be the case. Researchers behind the CEO Genome Project studied thousands of CEOs and found that 8 percent never completed college. This latter group were leaders highly valued among their teams, evidenced by the fact that 89 percent had spent their careers in their respective industries, building knowledge and cultivating key relationships.

I can tell you from experience that while there might be a traditional path for creating a successful company, you don't have to follow it turn by turn. I built a company that generates a multimillion-dollar revenue, and I come from a modest family background and never attended regular college—something nearly unheard of in India.

When I was 17 years old, my father told me I should help him run his business instead of getting an engineering degree. Looking back, I can see how that choice actually put me in a better place to become a successful entrepreneur because it taught me things I never could have gained in a classroom.

Valuing Exposure Over Academics

After deciding to forego college, I began attending a computer programming course offered in the evenings at a small institution. I immediately fell in love. I even paid $20 for a programming book—a price inconceivable at the time in rural India. After

I completed the course, I decided to start my own computer training center with four partners.

Colleges tend to create artificial environments where students don't get true exposure to real-world concepts. But in my own training center, I had unlimited exposure to creating programs and solving real problems. Had I studied computer science at a university, I would have been restricted to the assignments I was given and might not have realized my full potential.

Without an engineering degree, searching for a job in the tech world was a big challenge, but I eventually secured a role with Hewlett-Packard. There, I realized I had a knack for working on problems that were not easily solved. Because I wasn't chained to a college course, I could dive deep into those topics and build up my knowledge bank. Some of those topics even became the foundation for my future business.

How to Succeed Without a Degree

During my journey as an entrepreneur, I believe I've learned much more from working in the field than I would have had I pursued a college degree. If you want to strike out on your own and bypass the college process, follow these steps I did to build a strong foundation for your future.

Don't Study for the Test—Go Deep Instead

In most colleges, students have the system figured out: You pass the class if you pass the test. So, if material won't be on the test, there's no need to bother with it. Many of my early co-workers took a similar approach, putting in the minimum effort to gain promotions or simply not get fired. But in business, you need to actively pursue the deep knowledge necessary to solve problems as they arise.

Entrepreneur and investor James Altucher told a CNBC interviewer how, while he'd received a degree from prestigious Cornell University, when he got his first job, he had to take remedial programming classes for two months because he hadn't learned the necessary skills.

Altucher suggested that spending four years pursuing skills relevant to your desired industry is better than getting a broad yet shallow education through college courses. Instead of spending money on college, books, or online tutorials, he said that would-be entrepreneurs should seek out mentors to teach them the ropes in their target industry. They should concentrate on diving deep into the subjects they need to become an expert in.

Give Value to Individuals, But Bet on Your Team

College, by and large, is an individual effort. You get an individual degree after taking individual courses and writing individual papers. However, in business, there is almost no metric by which you can evaluate yourself that isn't heavily influenced by a team. When I started my own company, I prioritized building great relationships with my talented and trustworthy colleagues.

Once you've gained the skills you need, shift your focus to creating a team you trust to weather the hard times and support your endeavors. Instill in your team the mindset that each of you has something valuable to contribute and that each individual is expected to put in the same high level of effort.

According to a *Harvard Business Review* survey, 82 percent of participants rated leadership as a crucial entrepreneurial skill, so follow that advice: Ensure you provide your team with solid leadership. Make plans for managing your employees, maintaining company culture, resolving conflicts and communicating your vision.

Chase and Solve Hard Problems

As a software engineer, I found that one area I really latched on to was rule-based computing, a big problem with few solutions. Rule-based computing became a specialty of mine and eventually became the foundation for my company.

I could have never learned the depths of rule-based computing through an engineering course, though. I learned it through many hours spent solving difficult problems and exploring the limits of what was possible.

Solving hard problems became the focus of my entrepreneurial journey. If you solve hard problems, I learned, you never have to chase after customers or venture capital funding—they come to you. Early-stage VC funding has decreased recently, so it's better to spend your time and money tackling difficult problems head-on. Put all your effort into improving your process and developing your products or services, and your company will be more attractive to investors and customers alike.

So, take my word for it: Your failure to win life's demographic lottery doesn't mean you can't be a successful entrepreneur. In fact, the very reason you don't fit the mold might be what propels you forward. Don't let your starting place or your path in life dictate where you end up.

Use the tools and experiences given to you, and carve your own path to success.

ENTREPRENEUR VOICES SPOTLIGHT: #DEARENTREPRENEUR WITH CAROLINE STOKES

Dear Entrepreneur,

I am in a creative position, so I need to solve problems day-in and day-out. At my workplace, we frequently have tasks assigned and due within the same day. And while normally I can get them done in time, attention is only given to those who slip up on their deadlines. Even when tasks are completed early and of high quality, we get nothing. I've read a lot on motivation, especially motivation from a leadership point of view, and I don't believe this system of strictly negative reinforcement is productive or creating a healthy work environment.

I try to be optimistic by telling myself that there's a way to fix this, but I fall into thinking that I'd have to change the minds or ways of leadership of over five different administrators to have a lasting effect on our company's culture. I'm finding it hard to keep myself motivated to learn new things, and I feel exhausted and burnt-out. How can I take steps to change this "we need it now" mentality? Or do I just move on and leave the company behind?

Sincerely,

Crazed Creative

Dear Crazed Creative,

First of all, you have excellent awareness of the basic law of positive reinforcement. You know what the ideal work scenario looks like. Your current situation is common for professionals in service-based organizations: Management gets caught in a cycle of "pain avoidance" rather than appreciating all the good that's happening. Instead of affirming and rewarding positive behaviors, leaders are worried about all the things that could go wrong. It's no wonder you're feeling burnt out.

Let me commend you on your strategic and emotional awareness. You are continuing to perform well, even at significant cost to your professional happiness. Know that you're not alone, and there is a way forward. Whenever I coach people in this predicament, I offer the following next steps for consideration:

Step 1. Let's imagine for a second that you have the energy to tackle this at its core. Identify the most influential person at your organization and approach them with your concern. Support your perspective with data, or conduct your own research and present it to this leader. Suggest that a new model is needed, one which will serve the long-term health and wealth of the company and its employees. Remind this leader how important retention of key players is to the organization's success.

Step 2. Use your face time with management to present the alternate way forward. Come prepared with changes you would like to see and a plan to implement them. The leader may not ask for this, but you'll be ready if they do. Your handling of this tough conversation and presentation of solutions will demonstrate strong leadership and can set you up to be a real changemaker in the company.

Of course, this could backfire if the management team members don't share your opinion. This leads to your third step.

Step 3. Develop an exit strategy. Know that even if you do end up leaving your company, it matters that you took the time and energy to work steps one and two. Now when you're interviewing for your next position and are asked, 'Why did you leave your former company?' you can explain the burnout culture and how you tried to lead the company to change. You'll tell the interviewer how you gave your employer the opportunity to make the environment a better place. When steps to develop positive culture change were not carefully considered for implementation, you decided to seek a company that cares for its employees as much as it cares about meeting deadlines.

The right employer will be impressed with your high delivery standards and your initiative. They will see your clear leadership potential—that you're not content to just sit and grumble about less-than-ideal scenarios, but that you're willing to stick your neck out and suggest positive change for the good of all.

Let's talk about you and your career.

From a career perspective, consider your industry. Is burnout common? Have you looked at other companies to see if they operate differently than your current organization?

You mentioned that you don't have the energy to learn new things right now. Consider that a sign that you may not be ready to interview yet. I speak as a coach who's heard many negative appraisals of candidates from hiring managers. The hiring managers lamented that the candidates were burnt out and didn't have energy to gain new skills.

Do you truly not have the energy to learn new skills, or has your current work situation limited your vision of what's possible? New situations and people can bring new energy. When you feel supported, you're able to tackle things that previously seemed beyond you. I suggest that before taking any next steps, you cultivate the time and space to truly tune in to your wants and needs.

What do you really want in this situation? Is it a transformed work culture in your current environment? Is it a new opportunity? Do what you need to do to hear your own internal voice. I recommend a vacation, but even an afternoon curated with intention—away from devices and filled with activities that bring you a greater level of connection with yourself—can yield significant insights.

Move forward with steps one through three if your internal voice has told you that you would really like to make it work with your current employer. Know that this internal

GPS system is accessible to you at any time, even in the crazed, negative culture of your current environment. Tune in and let it guide you forward—wherever the path may lead.

By giving more credence to your own internal voice, you can't help but be steered in the right direction.

All the best,

Caroline Stokes

Founder of The Forward Co., host of The Emotionally Intelligent Recruiter podcast, and author of *Elephants Before Unicorns* (Entrepreneur Press, 2019).

HOW I WENT FROM ENTRY-LEVEL TO CORPORATE LEADER IN JUST TEN YEARS

Elizabeth Closmore

The first ten years of your career are formative. They determine your lifetime earning potential. They define your career trajectory. And they show you just how capable you really are.

No matter where your career is, we all have to start somewhere. Like many, I started as an entry-level employee—an assistant at Rodale, a publishing house, where I answered phones, filled out forms and organized meetings.

I then took a job at Hearst, another publisher, where I started dabbling in social media and eventually defined the company's approach to leveraging this new medium across its brands. From there, I went on to lead social business strategy (aka social media) for Target. And about six years ago, I became employee No. 7 at a little startup with a missing vowel, Sprinklr, where I started as director of—let's be honest—a little bit of everything.

Today, Sprinklr is a unified customer experience management platform for the enterprise. We have 1,500 employees, 1,200 clients globally and we're considered a "unicorn" with a valuation of over a billion dollars.

I'm now Sprinklr's VP of product evangelism and partnerships (yes, that's actually a thing). I travel the world helping leaders at Fortune 500 companies put customers at the center of what they do, whether it's marketing, customer care, R&D, etc.

It's an amazing role. And while I'm proud and humbled to be a part of something with so much impact, I clearly didn't get here overnight. Where I am today is the byproduct of 10 years of hustle and the many lessons that came with it.

Reflecting back on my journey from entry-level to executive over the past decade, here are five key lessons that have laid the foundation for my success.

Roll Up Your Sleeves

I spent the earliest years of my career raising my hand, asking for more work and always offering to help—nothing was too big, too small, too mundane or "not my job." That willingness to dig in, figure something out and learn more still defines how I work.

As you mature in your career, you'll start leading people, followed by teams and then entire functions. No matter how much your career expands or your title is elevated, don't stop being a "doer." Good leaders know how to delegate and help their teams execute. But great leaders will also roll up their sleeves and get their hands dirty.

Fight Imposter Syndrome

During my time at Hearst, I advised distinguished editors on turning their content into digital gold by leveraging social to build their personal brands and the company's. At first, it was exciting to be at the helm of this sea change in strategy. But as we waited for the results, I wondered if I really knew enough to advise my senior colleagues on transforming the business and doing their jobs better.

Fortunately, social is a real-time world, and the response from our advertisers, the engagement with consumers and the traffic on our sites unequivocally showed that the new platforms were a major opportunity. More people began to listen, more brands wanted to launch innovative campaigns with my help, and within months, one of the company's first major social media campaigns was featured in *The New York Times*.

Just like you are never too old to be a student, you are never too young to be an expert in your field. While it's good to have that daily gut check to question yourself and your ideas, don't be afraid to trust in your experience, your passion and your own capabilities. If you're passionate about something— if you study it obsessively, and you understand it better than anyone else—chances are you probably know what you're talking about. So speak up.

Find Your Champion

I'll never forget my boss and mentor at Rodale and then Hearst. Yes, you read that right, my champion was my boss at Rodale and then recommended me for a role at Hearst later on. But champions are more than connections to identify new career opportunities; they're coaches with a safe space to present your longer-term value proposition. At Hearst, she didn't just empower me, she gave me the freedom to think differently and voice my own unique perspective, to come up with—and then act on—new ideas. Because of her confidence and trust in me, I constantly felt motivated and engaged. She not only gave me the independence to explore new areas for our business, she provided the support and platform to get the rest of the organization on board.

I can't stress enough the importance of having a champion. This person doesn't necessarily have to be your boss, or even someone from your department, but they should be personally invested in your long-term success. A coach who genuinely believes in your value and your ideas. Someone who will help you unleash your potential.

It's not just about finding a champion for yourself, but you should be a champion for someone else. You don't need to be an executive to be a leader. You've got good, bad and great examples all around you, start to define your leadership style by trying out some of those traits or actions you admire.

Be a Sponge

In case you missed it, I'm a pretty big nerd, so let that serve as a disclaimer as I discuss my approach to consuming and organizing information. I devour information in any format (books, magazines, newspapers, blogs, social, TV) and I am constantly inspired and informed by what's out there. I realized early that I have a knack for applying what I've learned—with referenceable examples—from one task to another.

But when my interest in what was becoming branded as "social media" went from personal to why-the-heck-aren't-companies-taking-advantage-of-this mode, I approached information and idea overload: I scrolled through this cool new platform called Twitter and took screenshots. I indexed the entire Facebook app store (yes, really). I printed articles on campaigns—social or otherwise—that presented ideas or opportunity. I made step-by-step guides for apps that helped consumers take advantage of social media. I tore pages from magazines and catalogued my findings in a massive binder.

This quickly became many massive binders (and yes, I'm a tech nerd so obviously they were also digitized), indexed by themes that I would constantly reference. The collection formed my unique point of view and strategic frame of reference that allowed me to derive business applications from a nascent innovative space.

What we'll politely call my "research" inspired new campaign ideas, cross-channel execution, measurement strategies, advertiser opportunities and in many cases, software and channel features that have been built to support these activities. The process of consuming, learning, drilling in further, being inspired, sharing, gathering feedback, getting a better idea, was—and still is—an important part of how I operate.

The best way to get better at what you do is through experience (see No. 1). The next best way is to learn from others. Never stop being a student.

Don't Get Too Comfortable

People love talking about changing and being flexible, but the reality is no one is good at it. We think that after getting a job or reaching a certain level, we'll just be able to do what we do. Unless the "do what you do" is constantly mutating and evolving your skill sets, then wake up.

No matter where you are in your career, if you want to improve, have a job down the road and maybe catch the early wave into a new industry, you need to expand your skills. Ten years ago, journalists were expected to write. Today, they're media powerhouses, as many handle reporting, writing, content creation, editing and marketing on their own.

As the job market and individual responsibilities continue to change, you need to constantly expand your abilities to keep pace, let alone advance. Use the doing (No. 1) and learning (No. 4) to recognize the new skills you want to develop. Being uncomfortable as you develop a new skill set will ultimately make you more valuable—it can change your approach to solving a problem and help you spot a new opportunity. By contrast, what got you here won't automatically carry you to the next rung.

If you're not sure how to get started, put yourself in uncomfortable situations. Take a quick course that's relevant (or not!) to your job. Volunteer for projects outside of your department. Sit down for coffee with the person whose role you want to have in three years, and ask them what skills you should develop. Latch onto something, and chances are it will open doors.

Careers don't always have a clear path from one role to the next, or one company to another. My journey certainly hasn't been predictable, but there are everyday threads that we ultimately weave into our own bigger story.

There are many elements of a successful career, but most stem from a core set of attributes: hard work, assertiveness, a willingness to trust oneself and take risks. And while the path from entry-level to executive may seem unclear or daunting, I can say that with the previously mentioned combination of traits and leveraging some of the lessons outlined above, it's possible to make the leap faster than you might think.

THREE TIPS FOR ADVANCING YOUR CAREER AS A WOMAN

Michelle Burrell

Nowadays, a candidate's acceptance of a new employment position is likely preceded by a quick company Google search or a scouring of previous employees' Glassdoor reviews. As a woman entering any industry, let alone one dominated by men, as most industries still are—you should make sure that your first step toward achieving success as a professional is to closely vet the company you're thinking of joining.

Sometimes, all that involves is a bit of research. Ask:

- What benefits does the company offer?
- Does it have a good maternity leave policy?
- What about mentorship programs?
- How many female leaders hold management positions?

These are crucial questions; and if the answers are lacking, they're information points you'll need to flag before you accept a job—even making them part of the interview or early research process.

Doing your research may turn up some not-surprising data as well. Although the number of companies with large female workforces is low, they do exist. For example, the American Heart Association's executive team is made up of 79 percent women. Sephora's is 78 percent. And Build-A-Bear Workshop's is 86 percent. It's important to understand, for whatever industry you're entering, what its workforce landscape is, and what you want from your experience working within it.

If you're a woman, then, here are three desirable scenarios you may focus on as you apply for jobs.

Being Rewarded for Your Merit

Meritocracy models at companies are implemented to enable women (and men) to advance into senior roles. Where I work, this model has allowed females across the company to consistently climb up the ranks and compete for senior-level positions—so much so that today, the company is 90 percent women. The women leading our team's Middle Eastern operations and our division in Japan, for example, both started at the company as assistants.

While men have also competed for these roles, the advantage that employees —especially woman employees—have had because they were able to use their initial, entry-level positions to leverage their career scope within our organization, has been exponential.

A meritocracy model allows employees (no matter what their level) to develop skills that can translate into more senior roles later on (e.g., adept negotiation skills, client resolution skills, business development skills). One of the more successful meritocracy-based companies out there, The Kraft Heinz Co., has built its brand success on its push for company performance. Today, the company has almost 40,000 employees.

If your company instills drive into its employees and incentivizes them to strive for more—then rewards them based on that ambition—that practice is typically a good sign that you can move up quickly. Some red flags to watch out for, however, include rigid structures, managers who refuse quarterly check-ins or don't give feedback on performance, and even a lack of positive reinforcement.

Considering a Lateral Move

Every woman's journey to achieve her professional goals is different. It may not be a straight line or follow a linear blueprint. Yet, there's nothing wrong with that: Approval of a nonlinear progression appears to be widely and unanimously shared by professional coaches and career growth experts alike.

According to The Ladders, a lateral move can actually lead to the fulfillment of your career potential. Joanne Cleaver, author of *The Career Lattice: Combat Brain Drain, Improve Company Culture, and Attract Top Talent*, highly recommends strategic lateral career movements as an effective methodology for employees and companies.

Such movements can benefit both parties. Cleaver says, "Companies retain qualified individuals and employees not only learn new skills but have opportunities for promotion."

To better prepare for a senior role, then, consider a lateral position. In most situations, you have the ability to apply your past skill sets to new departments (and sometimes innovate along the way). Additionally, by switching departments or even cities, you'll find new skills to learn and master. According to executive search firm Boyden, the most qualified people for senior positions are those who have a well-rounded perspective.

Beyond learning new things, moving laterally, and/or internally also helps you build company rapport and is specifically advantageous when you're at a company that's in a growth stage. If you understand how multiple divisions operate, separately and together, you can provide essential feedback to that growth process.

In all, it's important that women's career paths across all sectors be recognized and respected. So whether you're properly vetting a company before accepting a position, requesting feedback or creating your own path, it's important to always remember to ask the right questions.

Preparing for Success

Preparation is key; before considering any changes, construct a clear and concise outline, detailing your vision for your success. Start with a thorough self-assessment of your skills and be critically honest with yourself about your areas of strengths and weaknesses. Being armed with this knowledge empowers you with a concise, directional guide toward your goals, and an exemplary road map for professional success. Overall, respect your career path.

So ask those important questions of your employer, your HR manager, your colleagues. But most importantly, ask them of yourself, and you'll only grow from there.

PART I
ADVICE FOR THE INTRAPRENEUR— REFLECTIONS

Carving out a path for yourself in the corporate world isn't an easy road, but a worthwhile one. For many, working on a side hustle or creating a path to entrepreneurship outside the confines of the cube may not be an option. And for many, having the backing of a company with an established record provides the security they need. Benefits, paid time off, a 401k, and a strong infrastructure are all pretty good things to have.

Yet you may still feel the pull of entrepreneurship calling you to consider a lateral move. That's where intrapreneurship comes in. You can flex those entrepreneurial muscles in-house by applying some of the best practices of small businesses and startups within the company. To do that, know what you want—set a goal. Is it to lead your team toward new projects and profits? Or is it perhaps to learn the moves you need to make to change your career path from, say, R&D to marketing? Maybe you simply want to help bring a new way of thinking to your team. The intrapreneurial possibilities are endless.

To reach any of these destinations, you need to implement some of those best startup practices: set your course, build a coalition of trusted advisors, seek the buy-in of colleagues, create a plan, and execute it in a way that not only helps lift your personal brand, but also that of your team. You'll hopefully find that, soon, you are the star everyone wants to hitch their wagon to.

PRO TIPS FOR SIDE GIGS

The gig economy has been taking the workforce by storm for years, and intrapreneurs, stay-at-home parents, and students are turning to part-time ventures to fill a void or earn some extra cash. A "side gig" is essentially capturing the best of both worlds: the freedom and thrill of entrepreneurship and the stability of a full-time job. While the spirit of a side gig—and the way it makes you feel—may cross lines of demographics, education, age, or skillsets, we know that not every journey looks the same.

Maybe you're a full-time parent who refurbishes estate-sale and Craigslist furniture to flip it for a profit that pays for a vacation you deserve. Maybe you have a day job but want to sell your proofreading or web design talent as a freelancer and build your own brand. Maybe you're a college student who tutors high schoolers in math and science to earn some extra cash. Maybe you retired from the 9-to-5 rat race but decided to turn your passion for close-up magic into a part-time job to fill your time.

Now let's get serious. We've pitched the dream: earning extra money doing something you love and are good at (who could argue with that?) while maintaining your secure full-time job or other pursuit. But is it all it's cracked up to be? That's the first question you need to ask yourself, and the first this section tries to capture. In the chapters that follow, you'll have to consider the pros and cons of your current situation and turn that side hustle fantasy into practical, tangible goals.

Start with your gig idea, and if you don't have one yet, Chapter 7 will help you discover the right industry for you. From there, you'll learn how to navigate your day job to ensure your job security and help you leverage that position for more opportunities.

Plus, you'll read some on-the-spot advice written to help driven entrepreneurs like you advance their careers and make their side gig dream a reality.

From dog-walking to bartending, Airbnb to Lyft, and teaching to freelancing, the following chapters have the key strategies you need to earn serious cash from your side hustle.

TEN SIDE HUSTLES IDEAL FOR MAKING SOME SPARE CASH IN THE EVENINGS

Murray Newlands

Sometimes, a full-time day job isn't even enough to allow you to save money or pay your mortgage and bills. That said, finding the energy to spend your evenings working can also be difficult. You need to find work that's not as challenging as your day job and/or that allows you to do something different.

With the above in mind, we've created this list of ten side hustles that can help make you some spare cash in the evenings.

Building Chatbots for Companies

If you're reading this thinking, "I definitely don't have the expertise to create chatbots for big companies," think again! Nowadays, you don't need to have any coding or programming knowledge to create even an enterprise-grade chatbot. Thanks to platforms like ChattyPeople, you can create a chatbot powered by artificial intelligence (AI) and natural language processing (NLP) in a matter of minutes.

The platform offers a completely visual user interface and is free to start. ChattyPeople chatbots allow your clients to monetize their social media profiles while acting as customer care, marketing, and sales representatives without them having to make a huge additional monetary investment.

Dog Walking

If you work in an office during the day and want to find a way to make some spare cash in the evenings while being outdoors, why not take up dog walking? All you have to do is create an ad and post it in local shop windows. You could even ask your neighborhood if they require your services. Dog walking is not only a great side earner, it's a good way to get some exercise and fresh air.

Content Writing

To start your own freelance content writing gig, all you need is a computer and decent writing skills. To find clients, you can sign up to platforms like Upwork and People Per Hour. There are even platforms that are specific to content writers. While you may not make much money at first, the more clients you work with and the more positive feedback you receive, the more you'll be able to charge.

Babysitting

Babysitting is another easy way to make some spare cash in the evenings. While you'll be given the responsibility of looking after a child, often, babysitting gigs involve sitting around until the parents come home. You may even find that the little one is already in bed by the time you arrive.

Managing Social Media

Who doesn't love spending their evenings on Twitter, Facebook, Instagram, Pinterest and the likes? Well, social media management is a great way to make some spare cash after a long day at work. While you may feel comfortable on all the aforementioned platforms, social media management can be challenging.

To get started, you could enroll in an online course that teaches you the basics of social media management for business. You could then create a profile on various freelancing websites to find clients. Be warned, social media management does take some getting used to and can be quite time-consuming. That said, it normally pays extremely well.

Housesitting

Similar to dog walking and babysitting, housesitting involves looking after someone else's property. Perhaps your neighbors are often away on vacation and need someone to check on their house. Or, some people may want a person to live in their home while they're gone. If you're asked to live in someone else's home for a period of time, you could invest your evenings into doing some online work as well.

Writing Product Reviews

Brands that launch new products need online reviews to convince other customers to buy their products. Sometimes they'll give you a description of their product and ask you to write a short review on retailer websites; however, certain companies send free samples of their products so you can write longer reviews that may be published in the form of a blog. In addition to receiving free merchandise, you'll get paid for the content you write.

Sales Representative

Being a sales representative doesn't mean that you have to walk door-to-door trying to hard sell products to people. While you can make money doing just that, you can also do it over the phone. While not the most glamorous of jobs, some companies pay you by the hour instead of a commission, meaning that no matter what happens, you'll receive a regular income.

In addition, you could also host parties. For example, Pampered Chef and Tupperware are two companies that are known for having representatives that host parties either in their own homes or at the request of clients. They then invite their friends over and showcase their products. Traditionally, you'll only receive a commission rather than a regular income from these activities.

Data Entry

Data entry is a mindless and easy way to make some spare cash after a long day at work. The best part about data entry is that you can cuddle up on the sofa with your laptop and type away throughout the evening.

While it does depend on the company, data entry jobs are normally not very well paid. That said, the quicker you type and the more data you enter, the more you'll get paid. Traditionally, data entry pays according to the amount of data you enter into your designated spreadsheet.

Becoming a Virtual Assistant

More and more businesspeople are hiring virtual assistants to help them with their day-to-day operations. Hiring someone online saves them a lot of money on desk space, electricity, and so on. It's also a great way for you to make some spare cash.

Typically, a virtual assistant will be expected to perform the same tasks as a normal assistant and some of these could include scheduling meetings, data entry, responding to emails, and answering the phone. Depending on your employer, you may be required to write blog posts and do some social media management.

This type of job can be time-consuming and demanding, but with the right employer, it's a great way to earn some spare cash after a long day at work. You could even make it a full-time gig if you enjoy it.

Finally. . .

Thanks to the internet and advancements in technology, making some spare cash is easier than ever. Whether you want to sit at home on the sofa in your pajamas or get some more fresh air, the options mentioned above will allow you to make extra money in the evenings without disturbing your lifestyle.

WHY YOU SHOULD START A BUSINESS ONLY WHILE YOU HAVE A JOB

Jeff Bonaldi

Many people that I meet tell me that they dream of starting their own business. I always ask them, "Then why don't you?" They typically respond by saying that they have so many financial and personal responsibilities, they can't just quit their job to start a company, etc. Then I tell them my story.

I had an amazing job in the financial services industry and worked with incredible people, but something was missing. I had real-world responsibilities like everyone else, but I really wanted to do something I was passionate about. Life's challenges began to stack up: the financial crisis, a divorce, and many of my close friends getting laid off from their corporate jobs, just to name a few. After going through these experiences, I was determined to gain control over my own fate.

At around the same time, I saw the renowned British polar explorer Robert Swan speak in New York. Swan is the first person in history to walk to both the North and South Poles and one of the most important environmentalists on the planet. He lives through his heart. His passion for his life pushed me toward a change. I knew one thing: Finance wasn't for me. I spent time reflecting on the idea that if I could wake up every day and do exactly what I loved, what would that look like? I loved adventure. I loved history. And I loved incredible stories of people doing the impossible. I decided to build an adventure travel company that would incorporate these three components. I would build it on the side until it was financially stable enough to be my full-time job. My company, The Explorer's Passage, took me nearly seven years of working nights and weekends on the side to make it happen, but it became a full-time job in February of this year. (Full disclosure: Swan is now one of our trip leaders.)

Many successful companies started this way. Instagram founders Kevin Systrom and Mike Krieger worked nights and weekends on their photo sharing app. Their initial foray into the market was an app that was similar to Foursquare, where you would check into locations. However, it was not getting traction. They ended up changing their model to photography only and it became the success we know today. Having a day job gives you the time and flexibility to hone your business model and create a product that will be commercially feasible.

There are a number of advantages to this approach. One is that you are less likely to need to take out loans, as you can proportion some of your income toward building your business. Secondly, you are less likely to give up valuable equity to investors as well. For me, I wanted 100-percent control of my company! While I might have had to put in more hours than if I had a partner, I now have the freedom and flexibility I craved.

Only a small percentage of small businesses make money over the course of their lifetime. This is important to take into account when launching your new business. It's very challenging to survive the ups and downs of the initial years without a stable source of income, so you should plan your yearly budget accordingly.

The British billionaire and adventurer Richard Branson is a master at protecting his downside risk. He is also a big supporter of the approach of starting a new business on the side. You may not have realized it, but many of his businesses, like Virgin Records and Virgin Atlantic Airways, started out as side projects while he was working on a separate core business.

Here's some advice about starting a business on the side.

Find Your Passion

I was very fortunate to have had a great job. However, my long-term goals shifted to living my passions. You will go through tough times starting your business and I won't lie—it is incredibly hard. It was my love and passion for my business idea that made it successful. While the hours were long, it did not feel like work. Find something that you love enough so that you won't mind spending your free time on it.

Take the First Step

Many people say they don't know where to start to launch their business. It's all too overwhelming for them. Just put one step in front of the other. Baby steps are the key! Come up with the name of your company. Work on your company logo. These will get things rolling. The next steps unfold one after another. When you look back one year later you will be amazed at what you achieved with just a few hours of extra work per day.

Keep Your Day Job

There is no guarantee that your startup will be successful, so keep working hard at your day job. Aside from the steady income and security it provides, you will still have an opportunity to grow and learn each day and you can apply these lessons to your own business. I was fortunate to work for an incredible manager who had a deep understanding of risk management, marketing and sales. This helped me tremendously in building my business. Learn as much as you can at your day job.

Look to Experts

You're not likely to know everything from the start. I am a big proponent of bringing in support, such as mentors and coaches, to help on your entrepreneurial journey. Having other opinions will help reveal things that you might miss. This is the key to breaking through to new heights. I learned this the hard way. After my company launched I was having a very difficult time with sales. While I was determined to make my company succeed, I was trying to do it all by myself. I realized that if I did not change myself then I would fail. I then brought in coaches and mentors and asked them to take a hard look at me. I asked them to help me change. It wasn't long after that the sales started to come in. My advice to you is to seek out help. It can make all the difference.

The day I quit my banking job, I left to run a thriving entity. Because I built up my company on the side I did not have to take a leap of faith. Take your time and only leave your day job when you feel fully comfortable. Building my business has been one of the greatest adventures of my life. Every day, I get to do what I love. I did it all by playing it smart, minimizing my risk, and thinking long-term. If you are dreaming about starting your own business, I say go for it—but do it wisely!

ENTREPRENEUR VOICES SPOTLIGHT: INTERVIEW WITH JILL AND JOSH STANTON

Jill and Josh Stanton are the cofounders of Screw The Nine To Five—their slice of the internet where they help transform dissatisfied employees into dangerously successful entrepreneurs.

When they're not CEO'ing they can be found travelling the world with their little guy, Kai, or indulging in a tall glass of something stiff. We got them to slow their international travel roll long enough to chat for a bit about what it takes to side hustle your way to sweet freedom.

Entrepreneur: How did you make the break from day jobs into Screw The Nine To Five? What is your origin story?

The Stantons: Here's a funny story—neither of us have ever had a "typical" 9-to-5 job! I mean, I (Jill) *technically* did, but it wasn't the kind you would expect. I was a bartender for ten years, which means I was working 9 P.M. to 5 A.M. slinging drinks at different bars across Toronto and using my daytime hours to chase after a career in TV and modeling.

It's funny because I vividly remember so many conversations with my mom where she would beg and plead with me to get a "real" job, but I could never bring myself to do it. I just always knew I wasn't meant for the typical 9-to-5 corporate life.

It wasn't until I met Josh that my eyes were opened to the world of online entrepreneurship. You see, Josh has been a serial entrepreneur ever since he dropped out of college to work for minimum wage at a small digital marketing startup. To say his family thought he was crazy is an understatement— especially when he told them that he quit that job to start a business writing e-books, with the first book being a guide to improving the health of your goldfish.

I'm not even kidding! That was honestly his first business venture and it went on to sell a few hundred copies, further igniting his desire to follow this path. A couple years later, he founded a software company (with another partner) that was dedicated to helping bloggers build and run hundreds of websites under one main dashboard.

Fast forward a few more years and Josh and I decided to combine our strengths and start a business together in the skincare space. Yes, it sounds completely random, but that skincare site was the catalyst to us starting Screw The Nine To Five—a movement that has now transformed thousands of unsatisfied employees into dangerously-successful entrepreneurs!

Entrepreneur: What are some of the challenges for the solopreneur/side hustler aside from the usual "balance" issue? And what advice would you give to overcome/address those challenges?

The Stantons: One of the most common struggles we witness among our audience members is **commitment,** and I think it's because entrepreneurship is sold as this "easy" journey to wealth and success, when in most cases, that couldn't be further from the truth.

It's this rhetoric that causes people to dive in feet first (without *truly* committing to the journey) because they don't realize that it's going to require a ton of time, dedication, sacrifice, and a tolerance for risk, change, and discomfort.

However, the ones we always see come out on top are the ones who *never* give up, no matter how hard it gets. They are the ones who commit to making business a part of their life and instead of looking for "balance," strive for harmony so they can stick it out for the long haul versus getting burnt out, giving up, and walking away.

I think what people in 9-to-5 jobs don't realize is entrepreneurship isn't about comfort, certainty, or coasting. It's about creating something you believe in, showing up no matter what, persevering through the tough times, serving and loving on a group of people and creating a life that matters to you.

Entrepreneur: You have managed to scale your business into several verticals. How did you do it?

The Stantons: It's been a journey of ups and downs; we're not going to lie! However, the biggest thing that has allowed us to build different businesses in different markets is identifying the revenue model that works best for our particular strengths and lifestyle goals; and that is affiliate marketing.

The reason we personally prefer this model is because, for the most part, it requires no fulfillment or customer support on our end. We simply connect our audience to the different products, programs, or services we use in our business and life, and if someone chooses to click our link and make a purchase, we receive a commission. This ultimately allows us to focus most of our time and resources on creating the best free content we can to serve our audience in the best way possible, which in turn leads to the company earning more revenue.

Entrepreneur: When do you know the right time to officially make the break with your day job? Is it just an issue of having enough money? What other factors help you know when it's finally time to cut the cord?

The Stantons: For us, as soon as we had enough money to cover our bills for a few months, we were out! However, we think it varies for different people based on their ability to tolerate risk, create offers that solve problems for people, and get those offers in front of the people who need them.

Ultimately though, it comes down to your personality. Are you the type of person who likes to have a comfy runway so you're not stressed about money, counting every penny and making decisions from a place of fear and desperation? Or are you the type of person who prefers to burn the boats and go all in?

Different people are going to have different preferences and therefore perform under pressure in different ways, so the best advice we can give is to get clear on what works for YOU! Once you're clear on that, be sure you communicate your desires, plans, and goals to the people who matter in your life (and will be directly impacted by this decision) and then go out, execute, build an audience, sell them what they want, and turn your dream into a reality!

Entrepreneur: What do you like most about being the master of your own destiny? On the flip side, what keeps you up at night?

The Stantons: What do we like most? That's an easy one! We absolutely love being able to call the shots in our own life and design a lifestyle that lights us up. Case in point, we're writing this while in Bali, surrounded by other online entrepreneurs and watching monkeys chase each other just outside the rice fields—all while serving a community of entrepreneurs we love and creating a life of adventure for our son. What's more is, every step of the way we get to learn more about ourselves, grow, and transform into who we truly want to be.

Of course, it's never without its challenges though and what keeps us up at night changes with the different phases of our business. For the most part, nothing keeps Josh up at night (gotta love those laid back Aussies!) and if there is anyone who deals with that it's me, although, thankfully, those moments are very few and far between. If they do happen, though, it's usually based on what's going on during that particular moment in our business. So, if we're in the middle of an affiliate promotion it's usually a question of, "How is this going to play out?" or if we're in the middle of a team transition it's typically, "How could we have handled that differently?"

It's never just one thing over and over, and (thankfully) it's never an overwhelming sense of stress or anxiety wondering "what if." We moved past those moments after the first few years in business and now know that we've built enough skills (and a level of emotional fitness) that no matter what, we'll always be able to handle what comes our way. After all, that's what we entrepreneurs are all about, right? Constant self-improvement, discovery and becoming the best version of ourselves so we can make an impact in people's lives and never be at the mercy of a 9-to-5 job.

THAT is what Screw The Nine To Five is all about and it's a message we will continue to spread for as long as we live!

Entrepreneur Voices Spotlight: Interview with Jill and Josh Stanton

CAREER-MINDED MILLENNIALS SHOULD THINK TWICE BEFORE STARTING A SIDE HUSTLE

William Harris

I'm a millennial.

There. I said it. I was born in 1984, so I'm right on the generational edge, and most of us don't really like to admit that we're actually millennials. I miss the cutoff for Xennial by one year. I'm just a plain ol' millennial.

And like most of my peers, I've had side hustles throughout my professional career. I've even managed to turn that side-hustle into a full-time gig running an ecommerce marketing agency.

But not everyone is as happy about our moonlighting as we are.

According to Barbara Paldus, founder and CEO of Mylah Beauty, "[It] depends on the seniority of employees and the nature of the side-hustle. If they are supporting their aging parents' business or are a senior executive supporting young entrepreneurs, then I would absolutely support it, especially if they are performing at their current job. However, if the side hustle is taking away from their productivity or is competitive with their job, then absolutely not!" Her feeling is fairly common, as it turns out.

How Employers See It

At a high level, employers want to know, "Will it take away from the thing I'm paying you to do?" And that's fair to ask. However, it seems like there's a lot more going on behind the scenes of different companies' policies on side hustles.

Jeremy Neren, CEO of GrocerKey, states, "I support GrocerKey employees having a side hustle because I believe that it's in a company's best interest to endorse employee growth. By supporting their growth, you earn their respect and in turn get higher quality work from them in addition to building company morale."

I've talked with a lot of startup founders, and even asked this question on LinkedIn, and this seems to be the consensus with most of them.

Another great example of this thought process is from Brian Wallace, founder of NowSourcing. com, who stated that he's, "100 percent in support of employees having a side-hustle! As long as it doesn't directly compete with their day job of employment, it's very healthy to have your employees pursue their dreams of exploring different types of work and industries. Several of our employees currently do this and it contributes well to their professional development, work-life balance, and job flexibility!"

In the startup world, this makes a lot of sense. Most startups were created by people that were working on a side-hustle on nights and weekends while working a paying full-time gig. Why wouldn't they want to support the very thing that afforded them the success they now have?

Larry Kim, who recently sold his marketing agency, WordStream for $150M, and now runs a startup, MobileMonkey, agreed with this—with one caveat.

"An employer doesn't have any right to your time outside of work hours, so from that perspective, I see no issue if someone wants to go to night school or make some extra money or whatever. However, if it was being worked on during regular work hours, and/or interfering with normal business work, I wouldn't tolerate it."

That's an important distinction and one that's often overlooked by many people. Having a side hustle needs to truly be "on the side." It's not something you should be doing while you're also getting paid at your day job. But, if you go further up the chain, from startup to Fortune 500 company, the side hustle is a bit less accepted.

When I asked executives and owners of companies that are valued over $1 billion none wanted to go on record saying that they forbid them, but it felt obvious that they aren't in favor of them. It seems that as companies mature, they're looking for a more committed relationship. And that's the best way to look at this—as a relationship.

When you're young, you're a bit more carefree. You might have a new girlfriend or boyfriend every three weeks (and your longest relationship is three months). Startups are also young, and they love that carefree, "wanderlust" spirit about you. They aren't looking for a ten-year commitment.

But as you get older, you tend to want to find someone you can "settle down with." You want someone who is committed to you and only you. You want someone who wants to build their life with you and grow old with you.

That's the same for the more prominent, more mature businesses. They've grown up, and they're looking for commitment. They aren't saying you're a terrible person for wanting to live freely, but they've moved past that. They want you to want to build your career with them and focus exclusively on them.

That being said, there's a growing push to change the stigma of side hustles within corporate America as well.

"For obvious reasons, the corporate world doesn't foster their employees to have a side hustle— they already have a lot on their plates," says Ryan Patel, former VP of global development at Pinkberry. "But, if the side hustle somehow benefits the individual, such as guest speaking or giving back to the community, corporations should make a change and not only allow for side hustles but highly encourage them. I'm not suggesting they dedicate an additional 40 hours to their week, but having a creative outlet will strengthen the best minds in their companies."

How Millennials See It

We got screwed. When I graduated as a registered nurse in 2005, everyone said I would never have to worry about a job because the demand for nurses was so high. Then 2008 happened and I was the low man on the totem pole. I was laid off for a bit and went back to school for marketing to diversify my skill set.

Side hustles are how I kept food on the table.

We can bellyache about how hard it is to find a job after college, or about how the high cost of living makes it hard to survive on an entry-level salary. Catherine Baab-Muguira does a fantastic job of summing it up: Millennials are obsessed with side hustles because that is all we've got.

Telling a millennial that you don't support their side-hustle feels a bit controlling to us and sounds a lot like you don't care about our general well-being. I know that's not true, but that's how we feel, and it's based on real-life situations, not prognostication.

So does it matter? Well, it depends on what type of job you're looking for.

Even if your boss says it's OK, a millennial determined to climb the ladder at a more traditional, corporate business should probably think twice about having a side hustle. On the other hand, if you work for a startup, go ahead and jump in once you've cleared it with your workaholic, eccentric founder.

Either way, the key is to figure out where you want to go and make sure the choices you make lead you down the right path.

FIVE WAYS TO KICKSTART YOUR SIDE HUSTLE WHILE LEVERAGING YOUR 9-TO-5

Erica Liu Williams

Jump-starting your side hustle is no easy task. Between managing your day job to carving out the time to work on your idea, it can feel like a constant uphill battle. When I decided to launch my healthy granola business granola, I was working full-time at Intuit, managing a team of five, and commuting three hours.

While many people see a full-time job as an obstacle to starting a side business, I took advantage of the resources, tools, and my network to make sure I was positioned to succeed before taking the leap. For those of you looking to transition your side gig into your full-time career, here are my best tips for not just managing—but actually leveraging— your 9-5 to get that side hustle off of the ground.

Get Feedback from Coworkers

Make sure to get as much feedback as possible prior to launching your idea and take advantage of the network you have at your day job. When I was formulating my initial gr8nola flavors for launch, I got tons of positive feedback from my family and friends, but I knew they were naturally biased and had similar tastes as me. I had to branch out, and leveraging my coworkers was the fastest way to get third-party validation for the product. Added bonus: Many of them became my first (and repeat) customers!

Use Your Corporate Benefits

Become familiar with the corporate benefits your company offers and find creative ways to utilize them for both your full-time job and side hustle. Ask your HR department if they provide access or discounts to premium resources, business management tools or training. Some organizations offer education budgets; use those resources to get ahead in both your 9-5 and your 5-9.

Not sure where to start? Pick up a few business books or enroll in an online course. Even if your company doesn't provide educational reimbursements, you can find plenty of online courses that are affordable or even free.

Leverage a Coworker's Expertise

When you're starting a side hustle, you're going to have to wear every single hat. I knew Instagram was going to be critical for building up the gr8nola brand, but I had no idea where to start. The first person I tapped for help was the social media marketer at work. Not only was she eager to help, but this drew us closer as colleagues and yielded another surprising benefit for my day job: deeper empathy for that department and an intrinsic desire to help others in return.

Use Your Runway

The nice thing about having a full-time job when you start a side hustle is not having to worry about your next paycheck. Use this as your runway to figure out what it will take to get your side hustle off the ground. In order to take the leap, do you need to hit a certain number of customers, revenue, or break-even? Or a specific amount of money saved or level of confidence to go full-time? For me, it was more of the latter, and I didn't take the leap until I hit those milestones.

Borrow Tools and Processes

So many of the tools and processes I use in my business are from my corporate career. That includes everything from setting goals with OKRs (Objectives and Key Results) to prioritization frameworks to specific collaboration tools I used at work. It's so critical to set up processes before you scale, and there's no better time than during your side hustle stage to take a page out of your employer's playbook when it's fresh.

This all goes without saying: Make sure to fulfill your responsibilities at your corporate job first, then crush the side hustle. The last thing you want is to leave a poor impression with your (hopefully) soon-to-be-ex-employer. Also be prepared to endure this limbo stage for a couple of years, if not more, depending on your traction and risk tolerance. It took me over four years to go full-time on gr8nola, but looking back, I wouldn't change a thing because

I know that all the experience, knowledge, and the network I acquired from my corporate career is the reason why I've come this far with my business today.

ENTREPRENEUR VOICES SPOTLIGHT: #DEARENTREPRENEUR WITH LAURA PENNINGTON BRIGGS

Dear Entrepreneur,

I'm thinking of starting my own side business so I can save up for big expenses down the line (buying a house, a new car, etc.). My significant other and I work decent jobs (enough to pay the bills), but I have this itch to forge something of my own. Plus, we want to plan for the future and make sure all our ducks are in a row. I just want to make sure it's a good idea before committing to anything major.

Is there any reason a side gig would NOT be a good idea? Would I be overextending myself to the point of exhaustion? Could I possibly pay more in taxes and self-employed expenses if I take on a part-time job on top of my regular, day-job salary? Is there really enough time in the day to maintain something like this?

I feel like I've got analysis paralysis, but I want to make sure I'm ready. Am I overthinking it? What's your advice?

Thanks in advance,

Paranoid Planner

Dear Paranoid Planner,

A side hustle is a great way to earn additional income or even build a business that could be scaled in the future. There are a few challenges with running a side hustle. Balancing both a day job and side hustle gives you more flexibility in terms of what your side gig looks like, but as with all choices in life, there are pros and cons.

As a self-employed side hustle owner, you'll have to pay taxes on your own for any amount earned over $600. This means filing a separate form on your tax return likely with information received from 1099s. These documents are how your clients or third-party applications track your earnings, and they report this to the IRS each year. You'd also report any income in your business earned under $600 if your business revenue was above $600, too, but your client might not send you a 1099 for that amount.

You could also bump you and your partner into another tax bracket depending on your current income and situation, so talk it over with your CPA to see if there's a dollar amount you should be prepared for; most side hustles will not generate substantial income if they are part time. However, many business owners recommend setting aside 25 to 30 percent of everything you earn in your side hustle so that you can pay taxes. Businesses/side hustle owners should pay estimated taxes quarterly, and your accountant can provide you with those forms since it's also much easier to pay as you go along.

Finally, you have to have the time and energy to maintain your side hustle. The first year I built my side business, I worked anywhere from 10 to 25 hours per week on my part-time side hustle. Having that foundation definitely made it easier for me when it was time to leave my day job, but there were times it was exhausting—and I worked plenty of nights and weekends to get the work done. There is an upside to approaching your business in this way, though; you can figure out whether or not you have a proven concept before committing to it full-time. Also, if you start a side hustle you don't love, you can jump ship and choose another one much more easily after a couple of months than if you had committed to it full time.

Setting aside a specific schedule outside of your working hours can help you stay focused on your side-hustle goals while not burning yourself out. It will be much easier to commit five to ten hours first and then scale up your business from there if it's something that is working for your schedule. Some people specifically choose to limit their side hustle to a certain number of hours or clients to help maintain some sense of balance. Depending on what you choose as your side gig, this might require being quite picky about who you work with and when! If you only have five hours free per week, make sure that as big a portion of these as possible is spent on revenue-generating tasks.

Of course, you'll also need to coordinate with any family members about your schedule if it affects childcare or other similar issues.

Staying motivated with the reason why you're pushing yourself, such as to pay down debt or even to leave your day job eventually, can help you when you're feeling a bit tired. Owning a business or doing a side hustle will always pull some of your attention and energy, but staying focused on your big "why" can help you reflect back.

Sincerely,

Laura Pennington Briggs

TEDx speaker, host of Better Biz Academy, and author of *Start Your Own Freelance Writing Business, Second Edition* (Entrepreneur Press, 2019).

I BUILT MY SIDE-HUSTLE WHILE WORKING A FULL-TIME JOB AND SO CAN YOU

Raj Jana

Side hustles are a low-risk way to earn extra cash or explore a passion—and there's always the chance they could become full time.

I launched mine in 2015 alongside my full-time job as a petroleum engineer. Back then, I had $50K of student debt, a long-distance relationship and parents who needed my support. I wanted more freedom, money, and control in my life, so I bought a few courses and taught myself how to sell products online.

Within 11 months, my side hustle was generating more than $250K a month. Last July, I quit my corporate job, closed the gap with my girlfriend, and became a full-time entrepreneur. Part of this success was due to a good product choice in a vibrant market. An even bigger chunk was because of the habits, disciplines, and mindsets I adopted along the way.

These are the four core principles that helped me build a successful business quickly while working a full-time job. Use them as you launch your side hustle to maximize your chance of success.

1. Build Your Focus Muscle

Time is your biggest obstacle when running a side hustle. With eight or nine hours spent at your day job, building a side hustle might seem impossible, but it isn't. Instead, transform "no time" into a huge advantage by forcing yourself to get productive with your limited time.

Focus is a skill you can develop and train— just like anything else in life. Combine high focus with prioritization and you'll become more effective. Eventually, you'll accomplish more in an hour than you used to in a day. Here's what you can do to make this a reality:

- First, plan tomorrow, today. You have a finite tank of focus and willpower, so you've got to use it wisely. It's a waste of valuable time deciding what to do at the start of each session. Creating a plan the night before so you can start straight away will make you more productive.

- Next, ensure you're always working on the most important thing by choosing just one thing to get done. When you focus on executing one thing, the small stuff becomes irrelevant. Maximize your time by leveraging the top priority, highest impact tasks.

- Finally, don't allow perfectionism to become another form of procrastination. Once you feel you're 90 percent there, move on to the next thing—90 percent is still an A.

2. Cultivate Rituals

How far and fast you go with your side hustle depends on your habits and your ability to focus on the right things.

It's much better to work on your business for 30 minutes a day than to cram everything into a single session on a Saturday. Working a little every day allows you to build momentum and accumulate skills that get better over time. When I was building my side hustle, I scheduled my second "workday" between 6 P.M. and 8 P.M. and treated it as seriously as my real job. Over time, my mind associated evenings with focused work. My output started to increase.

What you do consistently determines your results. Ask yourself: are your daily commitments aligned with what you want to achieve? It's easy to justify why you can't work on your side hustle, but when work sessions become a daily ritual, you can leverage your calendar to keep you accountable to your goals.

3. Brainwash Your Subconscious

When I started my side hustle, I had no idea if it was going to be successful. I had passion and drive, but no business experience or belief in myself to break away from societal norms.

I wasn't born an entrepreneur, so I had to brainwash myself into believing I could be one. You have to, because the world will happily convince you otherwise. There's so much negativity out there that if you don't train yourself to think you're bigger and better than your present circumstances, you never will be.

In addition to reading books, practicing a morning routine, and taking consistent action, I transformed my bathroom into a fortune cookie by pinning up my goals, positive quotes, and pictures of things I wanted to have to create a subconscious daily reminder of them. I filled my downtime with positive audio, listened to podcasts during my commutes and set up my social media feeds to only see motivational and inspirational content. I even started telling people I was an entrepreneur instead of an engineer, which changed how I thought and behaved around others.

You'll find it difficult to break out of the employee mindset unless you cultivate an entrepreneurial belief system. You'll struggle to take risks, step out of your comfort zone, and deal with the inevitable setbacks. You'll also struggle to retain success—even when you do achieve it. Brainwashing myself to believe I was an entrepreneur became the number one catalyst for my success.

4. Accelerate Your Learning

In the early stages of running a side hustle, don't try to figure it all out yourself. It'll take you longer, cost you more, and discourage you from trying again if you fail because you haven't built up the resilience to handle losses yet. There are proven methodologies to help you get your first sales, so fast-track your success by choosing a mentor and following their advice.

We live in an incredible time where we have unprecedented access to mentors, courses, coaches, and frameworks. I paid $2,500 for my first course to learn how to sell products online. It shaved years off my learning curve. Once I realized the power of learning from the right coaches, I stopped maxing out my retirement funds and invested in mentors—which further accelerated my path to success.

Once you win through someone else's guidance, you'll get excited to discover what else you can do—and you won't be able to stop learning and investing in yourself.

Building a side hustle goes beyond money, Building a successful side hustle will change your life thanks to the new experiences, insane personal growth, and freedoms that come from being your own boss.

But it's tough. Juggling a side hustle alongside a full-time commitment will stretch you in every way possible. It's the harder path, but thanks to the obstacles you'll be forced to overcome, the rewards are even more fulfilling. So if you're ready to build a side hustle, go for it. Invest your time and energy in these four fundamentals and use your business as a vehicle to stop settling and create the life you want.

12

FOUR TIPS TO TAKE YOUR SIDE HUSTLE TO THE NEXT LEVEL

Syed Balkhi

It seems like almost everyone has a side hustle these days. According to Bankrate, more than 44 million Americans have one. Having a side hustle is a great way to make a little extra money, do something you enjoy, and feel empowered. But do you dream of quitting your 9-to-5 and turning the side hustle you love into your full-time gig?

That's the ultimate goal, but it can be difficult to achieve. The daily grind of working a day job and coming home to work on your side hustle can wear you down. You might think you don't have enough time or money to turn your dream into a reality. So how can that be possible? In fact, there are some simple, low-cost hacks to take you from hobbyist to professional.

So whether you write, sell products online, flip houses or plan to start a podcast, with a little luck and a lot of hard work, you can take your side hustle full-time and make more than you would have working for someone else. Now, pull up your bootstraps and check out these four tips to take your side hustle to the next level.

Determine Your Goals

One of the first steps to starting any business is to determine your goals. You have to know where you want to go, and when, in order to keep your business on the path to success. Not only will setting your goals keep you more organized, but it will keep you accountable and motivate you to keep pushing forward.

Once you've written down your goals, you should create smaller but necessary tasks that you can complete in less than an hour. For example, if you have a goal of writing three blog posts a week, you can break down those individual tasks to create:

a blog idea, an outline, the necessary research, a draft, and a revision.

Get Organized

Another tip is to use a time-tracking tool, like Time Doctor, to keep you on pace. If you're the type who has all your ideas written down on notepads thrown haphazardly all over your desk, you'll need to get more organized, to create a successful business. A scattered mind will do you no good at managing and completing the tasks you need to get done in a day.

You can use a free tool like Trello to visually plan out tasks, projects and company goals.

By organizing all your business ideas in one place, you'll be stay on track and get more done. Create a daily to-do list as well as a calendar to track project-due dates and meetings, to make sure you're completing the goals needed to turn your side hustle into a business. When you know what's coming up in the pipeline, you'll be more effective at prioritizing and meeting important deadlines.

Build Your Brand

Building your brand is one of the most important strategies to take your side hustle to the next level and develop an identity for your business. Get a great logo crafted and create a style guide for your brand that covers colors and font you'll be using; then design your website around it.

Your brand needs to be consistent across all platforms, including print and social media. That's why it's important to create a branding style guide that you can refer to. When you make your side hustle look more professional, people will take you more seriously. As you're building your brand, visitors will form a connection with your business, which will look more and more like a legitimate business and not just a hobby.

Start Marketing Yourself

With your side hustle you might be doing work only for people you know, or selling to friends and neighbors, but to take it to the next level, you need to widen your audience by marketing yourself. One great tactic to utilize here is a website for your personal brand. Another: building your email list.

An email list is an awesome way to talk to targeted leads directly any time you have something to say, whether that consists of educating them with useful content or announcing a sale. The users on your email list are going to be the easiest to convert to customers for your business.

Another great way to market yourself is to get onto social media. You can reach a whole new audience for your business by promoting your business on Twitter, Instagram, and Facebook. By using the power of email and social media, you can connect with an engaged audience and skyrocket your sales without ever having to pay for advertising.

In sum, starting a business can be scary. But you've already proven you have the chops to become the boss of your own company by starting a side hustle. By following these strategies you can take your brilliant side hustle from a part-time gig to a full-time labor of love and become the entrepreneur you've always wanted to be.

PART II
PRO TIPS FOR SIDE GIGS—
REFLECTIONS

Way to go! You did it. If you're short of ideas for your part-time pursuit, you now have a stockpile of suggestions from online passive income streams to freelance gigs. You've seen success stories from adventurers to app creators to granola makers, and you've learned how to balance your day-job duties while you pursue that evening-weekend hustle. You've seen real data demonstrating the popularity of side hustles in the U.S. but also the staggering statistic that only 39 percent of small business turn a profit in their lifetime.

But ultimately, your success—and your happiness—as a part-time entrepreneur is up to you. Whatever benefit you're trying to gain from your side gig—whatever goal you're trying to accomplish—should determine where you go next. Is this building a business part-time your endgame, or is it just a steppingstone to your future empire?

Think about your current situation, set real goals for yourself based on what matters most to you, and then go for it! If that right next step is to turn your part-time gig into a full-time venture, then jump to the next section and take that leap.

LESSONS ON TAKING THE LEAP

We've all been there. Staring at your screen while having a full-blown case of the Mondays. You think to yourself, "Why don't I just get up and quit to pursue X or Y? I mean, if Jane from accounting did it, why can't I?" But the next thing you know it's 10 a.m. and your leading a meeting where you're calling the shots and assigning tasks—you remember that you are kind of a boss at work and that you may not be ready to leave corporate cold-turkey.

You're comfortable yet annoyed that you may not have it in you. You consider whether you're what they call an intrapreneur (someone who works like an entrepreneur within the confines of an office) or whether comfort has become your master and you'll never leave its sweet, sweet warm embrace.

Believe it or not, Jane from accounting had all the same doubts and what-ifs before she made the leap. Fear paired with doubt creates what almost everyone experiences as analysis paralysis or, our BFF, imposter syndrome. But here's the deal: You'll never know who you are meant to be if you don't take the first step toward realizing your own potential.

If you have a killer business idea, know that you create marketing campaigns that outperform your KPIs, have third level connections on LinkedIn wanting to work with you, it may be the right time to take that leap.

We've worked with entrepreneurs at every level of business. So we've asked those who've made the leap before you to share their experiences, doubts, and the events that pushed them toward entrepreneurship, side gigs, and the next career move. We hope they inspire you.

WHY LEAVING YOUR JOB COULD BE THE BEST CAREER MOVE YOU'LL EVER MAKE

Mira Kaddoura

Every week I get them: emails from women in the ad industry asking if they should quit. It happens so often that I've started to call myself the Quitting Coach.

These weary notes don't surprise me. Despite recent efforts to hire a more diverse workforce and promote women, advertising is still a boys' club. The women who write to me get passed over for raises and promotions. Their less experienced and less talented male colleagues get the prime accounts, projects, and job offers.

Research bears out what is obvious to anyone who has worked in the industry: Women who don't adjust to the grueling workweeks, inflexibility, and family unfriendly environment simply leave.

I understand the yearning for something different: I spent ten wonderful, magical years working for Wieden + Kennedy, producing work for brands like Nike, Coca-Cola and Powerade—but I started itching for new ways to challenge myself and take some risks. Then the universe gave me the nudge I needed to finally quit. If I was going to work 14-hour days, I wanted to pour myself into something I was passionate about building—something that truly valued what I brought to the table. So I went on to freelance and then founded my own agency, Red & Co., where every day I work to create a better version of this industry we call advertising.

The years after quitting weren't always easy, but they were infinitely better. They made me question, should I have quit earlier?

Security Is a Myth

The thing that overrode my instincts to leave earlier is the same fear that keeps many of us stuck: losing your security.

Here's the thing, though. Security is an illusion. Layoffs, client whims, an asshole boss, anything —poof!—and there goes your salary, insurance package, title, and fancy business cards.

But when you let go of this false version of security, you might lose much more. You could lose having brilliant ideas squashed by unimaginative clients, working late because of someone else's boozy lunch, or having to pump breast milk in a bathroom stall.

Instead of questioning what we have to lose, what if we asked: What do we have to gain?

Five Plug-Pulling Pep Talks

Still, the anxiety over leaving a "successful" job— even if it robs you of your personal time and relationships or involves "networking" at after-work ass-grabs—persists.

The women who email me about quitting ask the same questions. Here's what I tell them.

"What If I Fail?"

Good! Failure means you took a risk. Now use that failure to inform what you do next and view your ability to move on as proof that you're strong enough to do this.

"What If No One Wants Me?"

If you had a friend who stayed with a shitty boyfriend because she was afraid no one else would date her, you'd bring her a pint of ice cream and tell her to leave, like, yesterday. Truth is, you don't need an abusive relationship, and you don't need an abusive job, either.

"What If I Break an Arm and Can't Work? What If My Boss Gets Pissed And Blackballs Me?"

The giant void left by uncertainty is easy to fill with what-ifs and catastrophes.

But what's the worst that could happen? If all hell breaks loose, you can go and get another full-time job. The world will not end because you quit. This is only advertising.

"What If I Can't Pay My Bills?"

Quitting sounds like it takes your salary to zero, but it gives you the opportunity to earn what you're actually worth. Within a month of quitting Wieden + Kennedy, I quadrupled my previous full-time salary. You can, too.

"Is Quitting too Risky?"

You know what's actually risky? Putting all your money-making eggs in one basket. Quitting actually diversifies your income streams: If one project doesn't pan out, you have others in the works. Too many women stay in unappreciative jobs for too long, stunting their potential.

There's so much that comes into your life when you empty your basket and allow new things to fill it. Remember: The universe rewards the brave.

14

HOW TO TRANSITION FROM A CORPORATE JOB TO BEING AN ENTREPRENEUR

Carlos Gil

Starting a new business isn't easy and it, of course, has its share of ups and downs. Some months are outstanding (financially), while others aren't. Some months you're in "pitch mode" to land new business and others you're delegating work to be performed, hiring new team members, firing ones who aren't working out, and doing all the "things" that nobody on social media will ever know, hear, or see.

For a person who's historically been a "corporate intrapreneur"—otherwise referred to as someone who acts entrepreneurial yet is paid a salary as an employee of a company—to have full autonomy to show up and do your work on your terms while having the security blanket of a paycheck can be rewarding.

However, the thought of not having that direct deposit hit one's bank account every 15th and 30th of the month can also be terrifying to the point of paralysis by analysis. You may ask:

- "How will I pay my rent?"
- "How will I make my mortgage next month?"
- "How will I sustain my lifestyle?"
- "How will I be able to afford expensive dinners and vacations?"

These are all questions that run through the minds of corporate intrapreneurs—who have an entrepreneurial mindset—and lead them to stay put more often than not.

It's fear. It's self-doubt. And it's real.

On Oct. 1, 2018, when my LinkedIn inbox became flooded with "Congrats on your work anniversary!" messages, I took a moment to reflect on what it took for me to walk away from a job that previously paid me over $150,000 per year.

For beginners, working a full-time job with a salary and benefits isn't a bad thing if you look at it from the perspective of you're being paid to learn new tasks and gain experience which you will take with you for the rest of your career. Experience which someday you can charge large sums of money for.

Post-recession, circa 2012, I had to temporarily step away from being self-employed and go work for corporations to rebuild my credit and save up money, which had been nonexistent in the previous four-year period.

One of those jobs led me to start working in social media for Winn-Dixie, one of the largest supermarket chains in the U.S.; the other was working at LinkedIn, which relocated my family and me to San Francisco and opened a new world of opportunities which previously didn't exist.

However, there comes the point when the paycheck, company logo, or work culture does not fulfill your needs, and you have to assess whether your purpose and passion are more important than a paycheck.

If you've been contemplating ditching your 9-to-5 for self-employment, here are five things that will make your transition easier in the long-term:

1. *Have a bigger objective in mind outside of your day job.* If you cannot answer that you love your

job, then you're in the wrong position. I often meet gainfully employed professionals who dislike their boss or the company that they work for but feel that staying put outweighs the risk of going elsewhere—including on their own. If you have years of experience and don't think that your value is recognized within your organization and are being held down, perhaps think about freelance consulting on the side to get a feel for what it's like cutting your invoices, sending out proposals and doing work independently.

2. *Start building an identity outside of your current job title.* As soon as you get the "itch" to work for yourself, make your priority not what you will do but how you will do it. Begin with building a professional identity outside of your job title or company logo. Many working professionals are known as "James at X Company" or "Susan from Y Company" because they've built their entire legacy around being an employee of a high-profile organization—which is fine, but there comes the point where you need to create your own identity independent of that employer.

Begin writing for publications in your industry as your name only—unaffiliated

with your employer or current job title. Start speaking more at industry conferences. Participate in online groups on Facebook and LinkedIn to grow your identity and thought leadership but also to network.

3. *Secretly network within your network.* For two years before I exited my corporate job to start my social media marketing agency Gil Media Co., I met privately with close colleagues to share with them my vision for "next steps," either at industry conferences or by phone. While you don't want to share your intentions publicly with the world just yet, what you do want is for your closest colleagues to act as informal advisors who may have a job for you (on a freelance basis) or can introduce you to someone that might be looking for your expertise. You'd be surprised at exactly how many major corporations are looking for consultants or freelancers with your skill set and expertise.

4. *Don't quit without securing clients.* Unless you're fired or laid off from your job, do not quit unless you have a paying client or two. Not having guaranteed income will bring you stress which will make it harder for you to focus on the basics of getting a business up

and running. Therefore, it is critical that you have income coming in from other sources before you become self-employed (by choice). You should also have at least six months of salary in liquid cash saved up to help you bridge the period between going out on your own to bringing in consistent business.

In my case, a year before leaving my corporate job I picked up a client (ironically from a free speaking gig) which afforded me the ability to save cash that would eventually let me walk away from corporate work.

5. *Document the process.* Sharing your story is a competitive advantage. Why? Because it's your story. Strangers will be more inclined to help you when they see someone who's sharing their vulnerabilities. I created a short documentary titled "Chasing Opportunity," which discusses the layoff in 2008. This led me to discover social media as a gateway to rebuilding and rebranding myself, which in turn led me down a new career path to where I find myself today. While my story is unique to me, it's also real and relatable.

As you're growing a new business, document the process of growth—and sometimes failure— through daily stories on Instagram or Facebook.

Leverage mediums like YouTube and LinkedIn to amplify awareness around whatever your "hustle" is. You will find that there's a world of opportunity waiting for you outside of your city or state if you see it. However, sharing who you are, what you do and what you want to accomplish is critical to unlocking it.

ENTREPRENEUR VOICES SPOTLIGHT: KLINT BRINEY

Founder and CEO of BRANDed Management

In 2010, I walked into my bosses' office with shaking hands grasping my resignation letter as I soaked it in sweat. My parents' voices echoed in my head, "You're quitting your dream job in a down economy. Are you nuts?" But there I was, about to quit.

I'll never forget that day, as it was one of the hardest decisions I have ever made, but it's also the best one.

I was fortunate to grow up on a grain and livestock farm which taught me about hard work and discipline. I was put to work at an early age, learning the value and reward of completing projects—putting up grain bins, plowing fields, roofing buildings, driving a semi, and painting sheds.

When I was 9, I wanted my parents to buy me a go-kart. Instead, my parents offered to match my investment in purchasing a go-kart. I had a little money saved up from working as a "hired hand" on our farm, but it wasn't enough, so my dad suggested we build one from scratch and use our money to buy the steel, parts, and a motor. After some trial and error, our two-seater with a Honda engine was ready to roll on the little racetrack we built in front of our house. My sister, parents, and I spent numerous hours making left turns like we were racing in the Indy 500.

I realized I was fortunate to have a forward-thinking dad who was good with his hands and, perhaps, not all kids had the same luxury. So, I decided to build a website dedicated to showing others how to build a go-kart so other families could enjoy the same fruits we did.

Having taught myself how to design and build a website I decided to start building them for others and created my first business—KB's Web Design. By the time I was in high school, I had perfected my web design skills from our farmhouse in rural Illinois and started reaching out to athletes and celebrities who needed a fresh web presence. Indy 500 driver Sarah Fisher took me up on my offer, and I took over as her webmaster throughout college.

It was during college that I got a taste for being a booking agent working as concert director for Butler University. I booked talent and negotiated with celebrity agents, bands, and venues, including sponsorship ties like PlayStation and the MLB. I secured national artists like The Fray, Jason Mraz, The Roots, and Ben Folds while managing a six-figure annual budget.

Eventually, I evolved my position with Fisher to include public relations and was brought on to the race team full-time right out of college. I handled the marketing, management, and eventually was promoted to my dream job as her Executive Brand Manager. During this time I secured an appearance with Former Secretary of State and presidential hopeful Hillary Clinton and brought the most media presence the 100-year-old Indianapolis Motor Speedway had ever seen.

While I loved my job and the security of working for someone else, I kept wondering what was next for me. I loathed the inefficiencies of corporate meetings and office environments, where so much time is wasted and I kept feeling pulled to work on projects I was interested in and passionate about, rather than just fulfilling someone else's dream. I wanted command of relationships and ventures that compelled me and wanted the freedom to let go of the ones that no longer served me.

As nearly 400,000 people poured into the Indy 500 sports arena on race day for the largest single-day sporting event in the world in May 2009, I made a conscious effort to really take it all in that year. And as the song "Taps" echoed through the air, I decided racing was not the only thing I was going to do. I could apply the same principles and experience I had honed here to professional athletes in other industries, Hollywood celebrities, musicians, and consumer-facing brands. I had found my passion in brand building and I needed to take it further.

After nearly 10 years with the racing team, I walked out of Fisher's office and was ready to start BRANDed Management—which would cover all the areas of brand building from public relations, marketing, web design, and management/agent work.

Currently, we work with a variety of entities, from Dr. Phil, Dr. Oz, and ABC's *The Bachelor*, to consumer-facing brands like GoDaddy and Kenneth Cole. We even placed our 14-year-old client, all-natural Zolli® Candy inventor Alina Morse, on the cover of *Entrepreneur* magazine as the youngest ever cover star in September 2018.

I hadn't thought about that day that I made the switch from corporate to self-employed—a day full of excitement and terror—until I sat down to write about what I would share with you, here. So I decided the best way to take myself back to that moment, and that day, was to revisit my resignation letter.

As I re-read that letter, a flood of memories came back, as if the time that had passed was merely minutes, versus nearly a decade. And it was in this frame that I also was able to answer the burning questions, we as aspiring entrepreneurs and business owners, must ask ourselves during this journey.

I was able to leave the corporate world in favor of being an entrepreneur because my parents gave me balance. Growing up, they gave me the freedom to be creative and take risks, while at the same time giving me structure and discipline. As I look back to my time before being an entrepreneur, I sometimes miss the rules, routine, and structure of a 9-to-5 job. However, the freedom to grow and realize different dreams and passion projects far exceeds the security of working for someone else.

To be an entrepreneur, you must be determined and focused. I've heard far too many times, "It's not personal, it's business." However, I've never believed that statement, and have always put my heart into everything I do. My results just reinforce my aptitude for success.

Being an entrepreneur also means accepting full responsibility in building your business and creating your future. On the days when things seem tough, I do a quick job search and see that there are always other companies hiring and, as such, the worst thing that could happen to your business, to your dream, is Plan B: going back to work for someone else. And I already knew that wasn't so bad. But it would be much worse to give up on something before even trying.

It's also on those days, where I take a break to step back and evaluate where I'm going, and where my business is headed. Over the years, I've made sure to allow for change and to welcome diversifying my business, as I did when we added events to our offerings, which now includes producing popular events at the Super Bowl, the PlayBoy Mansion, and music festivals. In opening myself up to expansion, I was able to enjoy career-defining moments, like bringing in the highest amount of media coverage the PlayBoy Mansion has ever received.

As a business owner, I've also learned to say no, that "I don't have FREE time for FREE work." I've learned to fire clients and invest in ideas, other people, and, most importantly, myself.

I have also found myself neglecting my personal life in the stress and focus of giving everything I have to my business. My moment of clarity came after running after one of my clients in a crisis. When I finally caught up with them, I was sweating, out of breath, and felt out of control. I knew at that moment I couldn't put my best foot forward and be a representative of my business until I started investing more in my health and personal setbacks.

The next day, I took a photo of myself and vowed to make a change. I decided my health and fitness was my newest client and I would give it the same attention and priority as any other client. After about two years of hard work and discipline, I lost 47 pounds and felt back in control.

As business owners, we are walking spokespeople for our businesses and if we don't look and feel our best, it reflects in our business. We spend so much time making sure our business is running, our staff is doing what they're paid for, that our clients are happy, and that we aren't just creating a job for ourselves but building our own empire. Sometimes that hustle can seem never ending. We can neglect ourselves, we can lose our pride, our confidence, our self-esteem, and even our desire to meet new people. After I started enjoying the results of focusing on my physical fitness, I knew there was one more thing that was holding me back—my premature hair loss.

Clients increasingly value young, fresh business partners, and I wanted to feel more confident and stay competitive in my career. I knew with all the brands I had worked with in various industries, there must be someone working on a new-generation fix for people like me. I found that in OneHead Hair, an innovative, non-surgical hair replacement solution. I discovered that they were not yet readily available in the U.S. and, always the entrepreneur and deal-maker, I came up with a partnership to benefit both of us: I would help them gain an American presence, and they would give me my confidence back.

With my weight loss, new hair, and a renewed passion for running my business, a bit of déjà vu came over me, bringing back that question my parents asked me when I decided to start my business: "Are you nuts!?"

The answer is simple: YES. You have to be a little nuts to leave the security of a great job to take a risk and try something that could fail. But every entrepreneur knows the same secret: It's crazier to go through life living someone else's passion.

We don't get another go-round to try our dream next time. We get one shot. And we're nuts not to take it.

FIVE QUESTIONS BEFORE STARTING YOUR ENTREPRENEURIAL JOURNEY

Megha Hamal

Every entrepreneur's journey starts with a story, whether an account of overcoming adversity or an anecdotal moment of inspiration found in an unlikely situation. When one digs deeper, they discover that these stories have one common thread: courage.

My entrepreneurial journey began when I took a leap of faith to launch my own public relations brand. Mustering the courage to dive into the unknown wasn't necessarily a new thing for me. I immigrated to the U.S. as a young Nepali woman to begin my higher education. To do this, I had to leave behind a family and a country torn by civil war. Looking back, I realize that this scary experience 15 years ago prepared me for my entrepreneurial journey today. I learned that informed, calculated risks coupled with grit is the necessary combination to achieve.

How do you know if being an entrepreneur is right for you? To find out if being an entrepreneur is the right fit for you, consider these five questions.

1. Why Be an Entrepreneur?

Each entrepreneur's journey is unique, even though there are certain qualities, personality traits, and values that entrepreneurs share. Therefore, the answer to this question varies greatly from person to person. Is it wealth? Independence? Social recognition? Legacy? A combination of these? Something else entirely? Take some time and answer it for yourself.

In 2003, when I was 19, I emigrated from Kathmandu—a city of about one million—to Hesston, Kansas, a town of approximately 3,800 people. Before then, I had never heard of tornadoes, *The Wizard of Oz*, corn dogs, or Mennonites. By the time I completed my higher education and found some success in the corporate world, I was fully integrated into American culture. But I felt like my career growth was limited. I knew deep down that if I did not take the risks now, I would regret it later.

I finally collected enough courage to leave my stable (but unsatisfying) corporate job to explore the unknown and scary world of entrepreneurship. I told myself: If I was brave enough to emigrate from Nepal as a young woman, I can find the chutzpah to start my own brand and leave a footprint—a legacy—that is of value to me.

Most people have taken risks in life, taken leaps of faith in one way or another. These earlier experiences can help you find the inspiration needed to build a business from the ground up. Remember that time in the past when you were bold and dreamt big? When you jumped off a cliff and built your wings on the way down? Become that daring, audacious version of yourself again.

2. What Is Your Story?

Everyone loves a good story. As an entrepreneur, knowing your story helps you establish your brand credibility. Being authentic and genuine about the adversity you experienced helps you connect to your audience and build your brand's reputation.

Consider the former CEO of PepsiCo, Indra Nooyi. She has shared the story of her journey as a young girl from India who came to the U.S. in the 1970s to pursue her higher education. She has discussed the barriers she faced as a minority woman in the boardroom, connecting herself to women in business like herself, minorities in the U.S. and the female workforce.

3. What Are Your Values?

Knowing your core values and what you stand for as an individual can help define your brand. Your values give you a sense of purpose and direction and can eventually function as an anchor for your business. What values lay at the foundation of your brand? Is it giving back to the community? Empowering others? Influencing the younger generation? Cultivating creativity? Something entirely different?

4. Are You Comfortable with Being Uncomfortable?

Entrepreneurs must be willing to step out of their comfort zones. Many entrepreneurs share stories about how this idea motivates them to learn new ways of doing things and welcome challenges. Once you embrace the notion that being uncomfortable is okay, you can move past your anxiety and diversify your experiences.

Before I took that leap of faith in starting my own brand, I spent a few uncomfortable months deliberating the idea of quitting my day job and starting out on my own. The idea itself was anxiety-provoking to the point of losing sleep. Eventually, however, I learned that being uncomfortable is a temporary part of the entrepreneurial journey that leads to personal growth. Being uncomfortable, paradoxically, can be a good thing in the world of entrepreneurship. After this realization, I was able to tackle my goals with renewed energy. The vision for my brand became clear.

As Arianna Huffington puts it, "Fearlessness is like a muscle. I know from my own life that the more I exercise it, the more natural it becomes to not let my fears run me."

5. What Is Your Legacy?

This question is more about the end than the beginning. For me, taking the entrepreneurial journey was about leaving behind a legacy, a footprint.

We often think of a "legacy" as something grand. To me, it is simply the notion of making decisions and choices that my future self will be proud of. When I embarked on my journey as an entrepreneur, I asked myself: What is it that I want from this experience? What is the end goal? I thought through this question and came to the realization that social recognition and the financial aspect were smaller pieces of the puzzle. The big piece for me was empowering women who immigrated to the U.S. with a dream.

Lastly, know that entrepreneurs must have a healthy relationship with failure. Failure is an option—it's how we learn and improve. This process takes time, patience and, above all, courage. As Michael Jordan said, "I can accept failure, everyone fails at something. But I can't accept not trying."

HOW TO TRANSITION FROM THE CORPORATE WORLD TO ENTREPRENEURSHIP

Solange Lopes

Transitioning from the corporate world to entrepreneurship is going to be one of the most impactful journeys you may experience as a working woman. It will change what you have been conditioned to believe and challenge you to grow in unexpected ways.

According to the American Express 2017 State of Women-Owned Businesses report, more than 11.6 million firms are owned by women. These firms generate $1.7 trillion in sales, employing nearly 9 million people. Thirty-nine percent of all privately held firms are also women-owned.

In other words, an increasing number of women are transitioning from the corporate sphere to the world of entrepreneurship. If you are in this group or thinking about it, here are a few pointers to keep in mind.

Start with Mindset

Many, if not most women, suffer from a lack of confidence as well as from the notorious "impostor syndrome" in their careers and businesses. As a working woman, you may feel like despite your accomplishments, your personality isn't adequate. Or you may feel like you're not competent enough.

I've personally had to fight the negative voices in my head telling me that I needed to acquire an overwhelming amount of competence before being secure in my entrepreneurial abilities. Like many women, I struggled with the feeling of not being "enough" or the fear of being "the only woman in the room."

As you transition from a corporate career to entrepreneurship, you should be aware of these negative mindsets in order to proactively fight them.

Work on increasing your self-confidence through self-care, positive mindset practices and challenging yourself to face your fears.

Be Financially Prepared

Starting a business requires money. This is especially important for women, as they face greater obstacles when starting a business. While they start more than half of the businesses in the U.S., very few women receive venture capital funding. As a working woman, having a financial cushion to fall back on lessens the pressure. While there is always going to be a measure of risk involved, being able to financially plan ahead goes a long way toward accomplishing your goals.

Remember that the best time to set money aside while transitioning from the corporate world to entrepreneurship is when you're still employed. Consider living below your means before quitting, reducing your expenses, and paying off or consolidating your debts. This will not only help you build better spending habits, but also grow a reliable financial support system through this process.

Mind Your Emotions

One aspect of transitioning from a corporate job to entrepreneurship that often gets overlooked by women is the emotional side. The many pressures of balancing work and life, as well as the significant challenges facing women in business, can wreak havoc on your emotions as a working woman. Yet, emotions can actually help your entrepreneurial career.

Entrepreneurship is a roller coaster with unpredictable ups and downs. This can lead to emotional distress, and even depression and mental health issues. As you prepare mentally for your entrepreneurial transition, don't forget to mind your emotions, too. Resist the temptation to get down on yourself for feeling such emotions as fear, disappointment or even anger. Instead, show yourself some much-needed compassion and learn to use your emotions to boost your entrepreneurial ventures.

Have a Plan

You may have a dream and many ideas as to how you can make it come true. You may also have all the motivation in the world to make your dream a reality. However, you may often be tempted to do all the work in your business as opposed to working on your business. This is where a well-crafted plan allowing for effective delegation will help you be more successful.

Understanding what I would need to focus on as opposed to what I would need to delegate made all the difference for me. Don't be afraid to have an ambitious, yet realistic plan that keeps you on top of your business and not constantly in the trenches.

But be Flexible

While it's important to have a plan, being flexible during your transition can also be beneficial. Many women won't apply for a given job or project unless they meet 100 percent of the requirements. However, in the world of entrepreneurship, a certain level of flexibility and spontaneity is required.

Consider that some variables may change, and unexpected situations may arise. It's OK to be committed to your goal. Yet remaining flexible as to how you execute them can actually increase your impact.

Network

As a working woman, you may tend to have less of a support network. This is due to the fact that women tend to rely more on their competence than their connections. However, networking is one of the most effective ways you can succeed in business as a woman.

Actually, it's the network you have built over the years that will most likely help you land new clients, deals and opportunities. As you move into entrepreneurship, remember to keep nurturing this network as you develop new relationships.

Prioritize Self-Care

Not enough is said about prioritizing self-care as a working woman and an entrepreneur. Women, especially Type As like me, very often neglect their own well-being for their families, friends and work. Yet, there are times when self-care needs to be your No. 1 strategy.

You may be tempted to go all in in your business and forget about that much-needed timeout. Instead of waiting for the right time to care for yourself, schedule self-care appointments as you would any other meeting.

ENTREPRENEUR VOICES SPOTLIGHT WITH SHAFAQ CHAWLA

Owner of Shafaq Chawla Real Estate
aka Ritzy Realtor

Shafaq Chawla is a full-time real estate agent in Silicon Valley. Her business tagline and social media hashtag Ritzy Realtor reflects the fun, luxurious style of her brand. After several years in various corporate marketing roles working on brand strategy, business development, and event marketing, she found that working at some of the most disruptive and innovating companies in Silicon Valley had lost its luster. Armed with a solid marketing background, a bachelor's degree in business administration with a double major in marketing and international business, she set out to find a career that fed her hunger for more without compromising the lifestyle she wanted. Chawla shares her journey to career freedom with us here.

Entrepreneur: Was there a defining moment that pushed you to leave corporate life?

Chawla: I wish I could say that I had a single lightbulb moment where I just knew it was time, but I believe it was a culmination of thoughts and events that led to the decision. I was stressed out all the time and unhappy with the work I was doing, and the combination was impacting my health in ways I had never experienced before. I remember dragging myself to work one morning and thinking, "It shouldn't be this hard." If I'm having to drag myself into the office, how will I feel ten years from now? It felt too early in my life to feel this way.

But, what do you do when you've set up your whole life around a chosen career path, from the college major you chose to your internships and years of full-time work, and then you realize you don't actually get to do the work you set out to do and don't enjoy what you're actually doing?

What you do is you start to think about what's next—what will make you happy and how you're going to get there. What will make the next 20 years of your professional life more enjoyable? That was what I was inspired to work towards.

Entrepreneur: What led you to choose real estate?

Chawla: My decision to change careers from marketing to real estate was the result of several different factors fueled heavily by the encouragement and support from my spouse, family, and a few close friends. It became clear to me early on that this was a good fit for me because, well, I was good at it. But my compatibility with the profession came down to a few personality traits and philosophies. If you're interested in a career in real estate, you should consider the following:

1. *Do you enjoy working with people?*

   I'm a people person. I've excelled in sales positions my whole life because I've learned that people find themselves at ease/comfortable around me and trust me. The trust I establish with my clients is the core of my business philosophy and something I hold in the highest regard.

2. *Are you intrigued by the real estate space? Do you have an eye for the aesthetic and design of homes?*

   I have always had a love for fashion, decor, and interior design, so real estate provided an outlet to also feed my creative side. I love to travel and often find myself drawn to varying architecture all over the world.

3. *Are you comfortable leading conversations and educating others?*

   I believe power is in education, so helping first-time homebuyers and sellers allows me to empower them as they make one of the biggest decisions of their lives.

4. *Are you good with details and numbers?*

   I've always been an analytical person, and a profession in real estate is detail-oriented and data-driven. My ability to pay attention to the details gave me an upper hand in hitting the ground running and staying the course.

5. *Are you prepared to generate your own leads and client base while building up your business?*

   Starting out in real estate, I had to essentially start from nothing and without clients, you can't really build a successful business without them. This is probably the greatest challenge for every real estate agent out there because without a lead generation plan, there is no long-term business. I've learned which prospecting methods work best for me, but this is definitely the hardest part of my business and a continuous learning process.

Entrepreneur: What do you enjoy the most about being your own boss?

Chawla: The freedom and independence. It's liberating, seriously. I realized when I made the career transition that I've always been an entrepreneur at heart, but I was restricted by the rules and "red tape" that came with a corporate job. Being my own boss allows me to have full control of my business, on both the operational and creative fronts, and really embrace my professional life as an entrepreneur. I love the sense of empowerment and knowing that every decision I make about my business is solely up to me. I no longer operate under a glass ceiling. The success of my business correlates with how hard I work, and no one can tell me how small or big my business needs to be or can be.

Entrepreneur: What would you share with readers who are on the fence about making the leap?

Chawla: First things first, find your passion and be ready for the challenge. It won't be easy, but nothing worth having comes easy and that is especially true for entrepreneurs.

1. *There will always be a fear of the unknown and a hesitation to embark on something new.*
   The financial instability that comes with being your own boss can be a major deterrent for many, but I truly believe that when the necessity is there, the means become within reach. You'll find your hustle

when you need to pay bills, your business will grow, and you'll learn when to have faith and when to cut yourself a break.

2. *Find your tribe.*

Look around and surround yourself with other people working towards similar goals. They don't have to be in the real estate space, entrepreneurs in any industry tend to have similar successes and challenges. Collaborate, share experiences, and empower each other to grow. Find the beauty in community over competition—there really is enough business for everyone without the need to undercut someone else's success to achieve your own.

3. *Don't listen to the noise.*

Don't bother caring about what anyone thinks. We are a generation of self-discovery and finding passion and meaning in life. If you decide to start your own business and realize it wasn't the right decision, that's OK too. Life is a game of trial and error; sometimes you get it right and sometimes you don't, but the only opinion that matters is yours. The only way to find out is to take the leap.

4. *Create a financial plan.*

    Being self-employed can mean that you only get paid when you close business, and often that can mean unpredictable gaps in income. The first year of business was incredibly challenging because I was starting from scratch and it took quite some time to build up the momentum. The world of expenses, and bills don't stop to give you a moment to catch up, so not only did I have life expenses but there were also thousands of dollars in annual business expenses and memberships required to be an active real estate agent. How can you engage in real estate activities to make a living without paying the association dues beforehand that allow you to engage in real estate activities? Hint: you can't.

5. *Promote yourself.*

    Starting a business requires a multi-level marketing approach to spread brand awareness and acquire new clients. Being your own boss means that all marketing, supplies, and business expenses are on you whether you have an income or not. Everyone knows that being self-employed means paying for everything, but you don't realize the true cost until you start paying for it. No free pens and Post-Its here, friends.

6. *Keep your head in the game but also find a work-life balance.*

It can be challenging to stay motivated every day, but you don't have a choice since there is no one else to fall back on. I am responsible for my successes and failures, so if opportunities are missed, I have no one else to blame. It may sometimes feel like there is no light at the end of the tunnel, but I believe true hard work will always lead to results so stick with it and don't give up. It's equally as important to find a work-life balance so you aren't consumed with work all the time, you'll eventually burn out and that helps no one.

7. *Plan for the future.*

Consider making decisions based on where you see yourself in the next five years. I set up my business and processes for ease when I hit the production levels I intend to achieve in the future. To some, that may be ambitious and getting ahead of myself, but I believe that is the mindset needed to actually make it to the goal. You'll get there if you're ready for it.

But most importantly, be hungry for business and don't quit. Those who make it past the moments of self-doubt are the businesses that survive.

Entrepreneur: What does the future look like for you and your business?

Chawla: I envision my business growing year over year to production levels of a top agent not only in my region but nationwide. I plan to eventually build a team (perhaps even start my own brokerage someday) where I can mentor agents to provide clients with a white-glove level of customer service and consulting. I look forward to the opportunity to pass forward the mentorship and education that was invested in me by others at the beginning of my career, and continue taking care of my clients who have chosen to work with me over anyone else and trust me with their real estate needs.

HOW TO TURN YOUR SIDE HUSTLE INTO A FULL-TIME GIG

Nicolette Amarillas

Few people are lucky enough to love their 9-to-5s, and more and more people are finding themselves doing something else on the side, either to add to their income or to feed their passion. Sometimes, those "side hustles" start to feel more and more like the "real thing," and suddenly these people are dreaming about running a business of their own. Sound familiar? If you're one of the thousands of people dreaming about turning your side hustle into a true business, you're not alone.

Moving away from a steady, full-time position to being on your own is the scariest, yet most invigorating feeling in the world. I've found most people consider entrepreneurship either unattainable or highly romanticized. The reality is that neither is correct. Being an entrepreneur is a ton of work, but it's also completely possible.

Ramping up your side hustle means long hours, it's always being "on," its wearing too many hats, but it's also incredibly rewarding. So, how do you successfully turn your side project or passion into a prosperous business? What are the steps? We all want the instant gratification but realistically, how can we make it happen? I can only speak to my own experience, failures, or what I like to call "directional pivots" and successes. There have been a few true catalysts that have helped me turn my two side gigs into full-time gigs. Here are some tips to keep in mind as you look to the side-hustle horizon.

Be Honest with Yourself

Giving up the benefits and security that come with a full-time job is scary, and sometimes unrealistic, but it's also dangerous to keep waiting until the time feels "right." Ask yourself exactly what you need to have before you can make your side gig your new reality. A good rule of thumb is to have enough savings to live for about six months without income, and/or with the income you already have from your side clients. You should also have a clear idea of who your potential clients might be and how to connect with them.

After taking care of the logistical considerations, try to avoid dragging your feet. According to the British Psychological Society, you are 91 percent more likely to accomplish something if you give yourself a deadline. So do it! Hold yourself accountable. Maybe you're not willing to stay at your current job beyond a certain date, or maybe there will be other indicators that will make you certain that it's time to go. If your current role isn't fulfilling and the passion is gone, it may be the perfect catalyst for making the jump. Both of my businesses came to fruition because of my own realization that I wasn't flourishing in my current roles. I wasn't the best, I wasn't seeing the success I wanted and instead of feeling defeated, so I changed directions. For me, the clearest signal that it was time to leave was that I didn't believe in the goals I was supposed to be working toward.

Prepare to Scale Your Side Gig

Early on, business organization and strategizing are a huge component of success. You'll need to limit stress and create as much efficiency and ease as possible in your daily systems. This could mean scheduling things carefully or using free software to make your work more effective. I try to divide the week into days assigned to different business tasks. Try as best you can to not switch back and forth between your different focus areas within the same day. Going back and forth between tasks that are not related is inefficient and breaks focus. Give your brain a break and keep yourself on one straight road each day.

Digitizing your work can help, too. According to Accenture, companies that use cloud collaboration tools with their teams improve productivity, have greater clarity about what's going on in their business, and save money. When you first start out, it can feel silly to keep documents in a shareable cloud space (like Google Drive, Dropbox or whatever option you like best), but you need to have the structures in place so that you're organized and ready for the time if/when you hire a team to support you. This is a good thing to play around with before you quit your main gig. Having the tools and processes you know work well for you ready to go when you make the switch can make ramp up time easier.

Work Hard and Be Humble

Your time is valuable, but as a new entrepreneur you can't treat it like currency. What I mean is, be prepared to put in lots of hours with minimal return. Initially, time may not correlate with financial success; this is an incredibly important mindset to remember. Your time isn't money—yet It's groundwork. Building a side gig up from the ground requires wearing a lot of different hats. If you want your business to succeed, you have to be ready to play customer service rep, salesperson, individual contributor and HR.

If you're feeling overwhelmed, break the work down further. Spend more time working on the day to day tasks, checking things off the to-do list. These are all working toward your big vision, but in small doable pieces rather than hefty overwhelming ones. Try not to consider any task "beneath you" and take some time to truly understand what goes into each part of your business. You won't have a boss telling you what's right or wrong, so you'll need to build a sense of self-accountability—one of the toughest parts of being an entrepreneur. Take notes about the challenges you face in each aspect of your business so that you'll know what anyone you might hire will have to cope with. It's your best chance to uncover important considerations and think about what resources might need to go where, down the line.

Surround Yourself with Smart People

As much as entrepreneurship can be a solitary job, especially in the beginning, it's vital to your success to remember how others can help you thrive. Invest your time in like-minded people. Take time to get to know others and their stories and create valuable relationships. So much of success is built from opportunities or inspiration from people we know. Find people you connect with to talk about your ideas, write about your ideas online and build a community that empowers you. Take advantage of those around you who want to see you succeed. You'll be surprised at how much people want to help!

The number of new startups and small businesses has dropped dramatically in recent years, nearing a 40-year low in 2016. The landscape has gotten tougher, which makes being an entrepreneur scarier. Turning a side hustle into the real thing is not easy, and I'd be lying if I said I loved every minute of it. But just as with most other big decisions in life, there are always lessons to be learned no matter what happens. Be thoughtful, take smart risks and see where your side hustle can go.

18

TEN THINGS TO DO BEFORE QUITTING YOUR JOB TO START YOUR COMPANY

Dave Peck

You've decided you're ready to take the plunge, quit your job, and get your own company up and running. You have an amazing business idea you are ready to launch. You're probably excited and nervous at the same time, which is perfectly understandable. If this is the case, you need to take a step back and remember that you simply can't walk into work tomorrow with your resignation letter.

Being impulsive could be a huge mistake so you need to create a list of the advantages and disadvantages you will face when quitting your job. If you decide it's still what you want to do, there are a few things you must put in place before you quit.

To help you get ready before your big day of freedom, I've highlighted ten things you should do before quitting your job and starting your own company.

1. Do Research

Quitting your current job before getting your company off the ground may seem like the best option, but trust me, it's not. The best way for you to get the wheels rolling in a safe and profitable way is to grow your business while you are still employed. This will make your transition from an employee to an entrepreneur a little smoother.

You can't jump headfirst into building your new office block or warehouse if you haven't done your research. You need to know that you have a product or service that you know the ins and outs of, that is unique, and above all, that will sell.

Background research you need to do includes, but is not limited to:

- Learning everything about your product or service
- Knowing your audience and buyer personas
- Researching your competitors
- Finding the right teams
- Knowing what your most profitable sales and marketing channels will be

2. Create a Business Plan

Once you've done your research, you need to put it on paper. Laying out a business plan before taking the plunge will be a key success driver. Your business plan will be something you will show to potential investors, partners, and other company stakeholders. It typically includes:

- An overview
- An executive summary
- A company description
- Your objectives, vision, and mission statement
- Information about the market and industry into which you are entering
- The strategy you are going to follow to enter the market
- The team you will have
- A marketing plan
- An operational plan

- A financial plan
- An appendix with more detailed information

3. Outline Funding Options

Before looking at funding for your company, you need to have your own personal finances in check. If you quit with just a couple of hundred dollars in your pocket, with rent, insurance, and your phone bill to pay, you may find it difficult to focus your efforts on your new company.

In addition to planning your personal finances, you will need to have a plan for your startup. You'll typically have three options:

- One or multiple investors
- Your personal savings
- A grant or award for your project

Either way, you need to plan in advance because if you can't get the capital to get started, your business will stagnate, and you will be faced with very few options.

4. Create a Structure

You need to have the structure for your startup in place before you can quit your job, specifically, your legal structure. There are various types of businesses entities you could become:

- A corporation
- A limited liability company
- A partnership
- Sole proprietorship

You need to consider:

- The operational complexity
- Liability
- Taxes
- Control
- Capital
- Licenses, permits and regulations

5. Leverage Resources

Of course, you do not want to spend money if you can avoid it. You need to look at the resources that are currently available to you. For example, you may have a friend who is a web developer; they might be able to give you special rates and work for you on a need-to-know basis.

You should contact friends who have started their own business and ask them if they know a good accountant, marketing expert, and so on. Think about joining an online book club to learn more about entrepreneurship.

Lastly, contracting all your experts could become expensive. Consider investing in online education for your team that will teach them skills, such as SEO, email marketing, and much more.

6. Leave on Good Terms

Quitting your job without working your notice period, gossiping across the office, not completing your final assignments, and not training your replacement could be the worst decision of your life.

Of course, you are leaving to start your own venture, but you cannot be sure that it will be a success or that your old company won't come in handy one day. Leave without burning any bridges and you may be able to cash in a favor one day. Your old employer may even send clients your way knowing that you are a trustworthy businessperson.

7. Sweat the Small Details

As an entrepreneur, it's easy to become the type of person that can see the big picture. Unfortunately, if you don't focus on the small details, you won't be able to mold the perfect company. Planning is key, and little things such as choosing the right social media channels, keeping up to date with emails, or even remembering to file your taxes are vital to your success.

8. Secure Office Space

When planning the day when you quit your job, many assume that they will work from home until their company is off the ground and they have a team backing them up. Although this could work in the short term, it's not a feasible option in the long run.

If you choose to work from home, you need to find a balance between your personal space and workspace. Working in bed, on your computer, all day, every day will lead you towards an unhealthy lifestyle that could have a domino effect on the progress your startup makes.

9. Create a Portfolio or Resume

You may think that owning your own company means you'll never have to create another resume in your life. Wrong! Bulking up your resume and/ or portfolio is a key driver when building your new business because you will need to prove to your investors, teams, and even clients that you are worth their money.

10. Finally . . .

Remember that starting a new business is going to be more challenging than you imagined. You're going to have to make the planning process your full-time job before you even see an income. That said, with the tips outlined above, you could make it the best, most profitable adventure you've ever embarked on from both a professional and emotional point of view.

PART III
LESSONS ON TAKING THE LEAP—REFLECTIONS

Making the leap from full-time employee or intrapreneur to be your own boss is not for the faint of heart. While some people seem to move from one career to another effortlessly, it can be a daunting task for anyone. After all, you are leaving the safety net that often provides the security of health insurance, a retirement account, and a regular paycheck. Some people jump ship every couple of years, while others may slog along in the same job for decades before finding the courage to leave. The leap looks different for each and every one of us, and there is no wrong way to take it.

We hope that this section has inspired you to start thinking about what it really means emotionally and financially to start your own business, make a career change, or run a side hustle.

Once you've had a chance to digest the wisdom and realities these entrepreneurs shared, you can start thinking toward the future and plan your exit strategy. In the next section, we show you what you need to set yourself up for success as you prepare for that giant leap.

EXIT STRATEGIES AND KICKASS COMEBACKS

When you know, you know. There will come a moment in your work life where it's time for a change—on a grand scale. Enter the exit strategy. Even employees with a long track record leave the company eventually. And that person just might be you. So like any good intrapreneur, you plan. And then you make it happen.

People leave their jobs for all sorts of reasons, but often it's because they are moving on to stake their claim in the entrepreneurial landscape. Whether the break is a clean one or you've carved out a parallel path with a side hustle, you're going to want to have a strategy in place to help you leave with a sense of goodwill intact and without leaving your coworkers standing in your dust.

In this section, our resident exit strategy experts walk you through some of the major considerations to keep in mind when creating your exit strategy roadmap. You'll read about how to prepare yourself and your colleagues for your exit as well as how to set up your finances and family for the big changes ahead. You'll also hear from some entrepreneurs who had to get creative with their comebacks and read about their best practices for making a smooth transition.

19

THE ENTREPRENEURIAL EXIT STRATEGY—PREPARE YOURSELF

Candace Sjogren

When you started your business early on, you were not likely planning to sell it. You had a big idea, a skill that no one else could quite match, a passion for changing the world in some way. And if any investor asked you about your exit strategy, you would placate them by noting the three giants in your industry, but would likely state, "But I intend to execute against my business plan. As long as my business is making money, there is no need to exit."

I wholeheartedly believe that nearly every founder feels this way in the beginning. But running a business is hard work. It requires untold hours of blood, sweat, and tears and has no sympathy for its founder's illnesses, family needs, or mental stress.

It is inevitable that you, founder, will one day retire or pass on (let's hope you have some easy days before you go). Knowing that you cannot run your business forever, and assuming that your company will be wildly successful, it is good to begin planning for succession earlier rather than later in your company's life cycle.

Follow these four tips for building good habits early on so you have an easy exit when you are ready to pass the reigns.

Form a Board of Directors or Advisors

It may seem a bit harrowing to set up a board in the early days when you are launching. Once you take on investor dollars, this will be required, but if you are bootstrapping, you likely want to maintain complete control for as long as possible. Inviting directors prior to a fundraise would unnecessarily create a reporting and decision-making structure that you and future investors do not want.

However, setting up a board of advisors and treating it as if it were a board of directors can be quite useful in later years. Structure your board so that your advisors do not have voting power, but offer them small compensation or equity instead, and treat them seriously. Schedule monthly board meetings and come to your board with a meaningful agenda around key inflection points your company will need to meet in order to succeed.

Organizing a board will help build accountability into your business model and will organize your business according to goals that can be tracked in the future.

Send Monthly Investor/Board Updates

Writing down your meaningful milestones is just as important as making yourself accountable to a board of peers. If you don't write down your goals and accomplishments, it is hard to prove, at a later point in time, that you accomplished them in the first place.

Consider sending a monthly investor and/or board update, outlining your successes from the previous month, upcoming inflection points and key hires and needs from your board. Not only will this garner favor with investors and show openness and responsibility; it will also give you a written report card to include in any potential acquisition package down the road.

Make Friends with Your Competitors

If you are in a cutting-edge new industry, you are likely not alone. And if you are spinning off from a previous employer, you know exactly who else serves your customer. You should not only do your research to know exactly who your competitors are and how you differentiate. You should also take the time to get to know each of the founders in your industry. Attend industry events and shows. Seek out opportunities to joint venture or create industry trade groups.

Should your company take a turn for the worse in the future, your competitors are most likely to seek out your assets. And should you succeed, you may want theirs. Either way, building strength in your industry through openness and communication can help you significantly at the time of exit.

Train Your Staff to Seek Upward Mobility

When we craft our exit strategy in our business plan or add the exit slide to our investor deck, we often look outward for a potential acquirer. However, companies are purchased by their employees quite often, and employee-acquired businesses are on the rise.

Offering stock to your employees builds loyalty within the company and helps you to diversify potential future buyers over time. Whether you plan on selling your business or not, you will want to build trust and investment with your team, and offering some form of an employee stock ownership program (ESOP) and internal promotion structure are two ways to build this opportunity for yourself.

In the end, you will want to follow the tips suggested above whether you ultimately sell your company or not. Building good habits now will only help you to succeed later, whether that success comes while sitting at the helm of your business or sending it off under new control.

HOW TO TRANSITION TO EMPLOYEE OWNERSHIP

from Finance Your Business *by The Staff of Entrepreneur Media, Inc.*

Kim Jordan and Jeff Lebesch wanted to run a more democratic business. Rather than shoulder all the tough decisions themselves, the founders of New Belgium Brewing Company sought their employees' input early on. This meant cultivating what Jordan calls a "high-involvement culture" of engaged, enthusiastic workers and transparency with staff about all sorts of matters, including company finances.

But employee enthusiasm goes only so far, so in 1996, the pair created a phantom deferred compensation plan, at no cost to the staff of their Fort Collins, Colorado–based craft brewing company. Later, when they started an employee stock ownership plan (ESOP), they honored the original plan until all account-holders' ESOP balances were larger than their phantom balances.

When Lebesch left New Belgium in 2009, Jordan and the company bought him out, bringing employee-owned shares to 41 percent. After mulling succession plans, Jordan opted for full employee ownership. By early 2013 more than 500 New Belgium employees— Jordan refers to them as "co-workers"—assumed 100 percent ownership of the company. (Shares are awarded based on the recipient's percentage of the total wage pool.)

The benefits have been plentiful. "We have great retention," says Jordan, CEO. "Our turnover is under 5 percent."

The employee-owners are not only happy at work, she says, but are also a regular source of bright ideas. Business is hopping, too. New Belgium, maker of Fat Tire ale, is the third-largest craft brewer in the U.S. and the eighth-largest brewer overall.

New Belgium isn't the only business thriving under employee ownership. "If you look at the numbers, on average, ESOPs improve performance," says Loren Rodgers, executive director of the National Center for Employee Ownership (NCEO), a nonprofit organization with more than 3,000 members. Three decades of research show that ESOP companies enjoy higher sales growth, higher employee productivity, more job creation and fewer layoffs, he adds.

If you're interested in running a more egalitarian company, here are four steps you need to consider.

Plan with Employee Succession in Mind

It's never too soon to ponder who you want running your company 5, 10 or 20 years out. "You're not going to own your company forever," says Alex Moss, founder and president of Philadelphia-based Praxis Consulting Group, which helps employee-owned companies improve corporate leadership, culture, and strategy. "You're going to either sell it or you're going to die owning it."

Contemplating who will take the reins when the time comes—and ensuring that all founders are in agreement—can save future headaches and heartache. You don't want to be forced to sell your baby to an investor or a competitor because you haven't thought ahead, Moss says. Instead, employee ownership offers a way for the company you built to remain independent and your corporate mission to stay intact.

If employee succession appeals to you, it's important to start running a more democratic ship now. Yes, transitioning to an ESOP or a worker co-op takes time and legal help. But a move to either structure also affects who you hire, how you manage staff and which investors you partner with. The sooner you adjust your recruitment, management and fundraising tactics, the easier the leap will be.

Open the Books

Although corporate transparency isn't a requirement for ESOP success, it certainly helps. "Our most successful members started treating employees like owners before they actually made them owners," NCEO's Rodgers says.

Jordan concurs. "I think people lose the power of feeling like an owner if they don't know what goes on behind the scenes," she notes.

That's why all New Belgium employees can access the corporate intranet "and look at the financials to see where the money goes," Jordan says. It's also why New Belgium managers share sales and financial performance figures with employees at monthly staff meetings and give progress and spending reports on big corporate initiatives, such as opening the Asheville brewery.

But you can't expect all new hires to know their way around budgets and forecasts from day one. That's why the brewery—whose staff includes production workers, microbiologists, chemists and salespeople—incorporates financial literacy training into its mandatory employee orientation and devotes a portion of each monthly staff meeting to educating the team on accounting ratios, cash flow, and other financial topics.

"It's a commitment," Jordan explains. "You have to say, 'We're going to dive into a lot with people. We're going to teach them to really get the benefit out of it.'"

Hire with Future Partners in Mind

Embracing a more democratic culture involves rethinking the hiring process. "We're not interviewing to hire an employee," says Blake Jones, president of Namasté Solar, a solar-installation company in Boulder, Colorado, that became an employee-owned cooperative in 2011. "We're interviewing to hire a potential business partner."

The co-op's lengthy screening process starts with one meeting to assess a candidate's job skills, followed by another to determine whether the candidate would be appropriate for ownership.

"We don't want someone to come to work for us just because we're a great place to work," Jones explains. "We want people to be excited specifically about our company model." In this context, the old interview chestnut, "Where do you see yourself in five years?" is more relevant than ever.

Also imperative: involving as many employees as possible in the hiring process. Besides helping to sort out the square pegs, this gives workers another layer of responsibility. "Not only do they feel like they are insiders and decision-makers, but they also feel some responsibility for making sure the new hires work out," NCEO's Rodgers says.

Cultivate a Culture of Democracy

Rather than shield employees from the big decisions, the most successful employee-owned businesses encourage staff to help make them. This isn't good just for employee morale; it's good for the company overall.

"When the people making the decisions bear the consequences and responsibility for those decisions and share the rewards, better decisions happen," Abrams explains. After all, frontline workers often see operational problems and business opportunities—and have ideas for fixes or new initiatives—that might not occur to management.

Contributing ideas may not come naturally to all employees. "You can't just take an employee who doesn't know a lot about business and expect them to be a good co-owner," says Jones, whose company has 60 owners. "You've got to coach them."

To that end, Namasté Solar's employees go through a one-year orientation period before they can buy stock in the company. During that time, potential owners (called candidates) are paired with veterans and encouraged to learn about the business and get more involved. Guided by their mentors, newbies must complete a 12-item curriculum, from understanding the corporate bylaws to meeting with the director of finance for training in reading financial statements.

Jones says the time spent grooming future co-owners is well worth it. "The investment pays off tremendously in the form of engaged, passionate, empowered co-owners who will think and act like an owner the way that you do," he explains. "The secret to our success is that we've got [60 times] the entrepreneurial spirit [and] creative, passionate motivation that a sole proprietor would have."

21

BEFORE YOU ENTER INTO FRANCHISING, CONSIDER YOUR EXIT

Jim Judy

Beginning life as a franchise business owner is an exciting time. Owners are often leaving behind life as an employee in favor of experiencing a new-found freedom. Perhaps they've been unemployed for a time and are excited to be working on something new again. Maybe they've always been self-employed and this is just their latest venture.

However, if you're that owner, you need to make sure your beginning is as good as it can be.

As a franchise owner, know that it's wise to consider the end even as you make your start.

Huh? you're probably wondering, because your eventual exit strategy may not seem like an important consideration when you're just starting life as a franchisee. But the fact is that one way or another, you and your business will someday part ways. Unfortunately, not enough small business owners are planning for that event.

And having the end in mind at the beginning of your franchise adventure will give you peace of mind that when your exit comes, you'll be ready for it.

Franchise candidates with whom I bring up the topic of an exit strategy are sometimes caught off guard, but it's a critical part to our conversation. As a franchise business consultant, I can't just be concerned with their arrival at franchising. I need to be sure they can successfully depart.

That's because the sale is where the fruits of your labor are realized. The years you spend as the business owner aren't just spent *operating* the business, they are spent *growing* the business, and hopefully growing it into an asset ready to be sold for a nice profit when the time is right. That time will be different for everyone, but it will come.

When consulting with franchise candidates, these are the key considerations we discuss regarding their exit strategy.

How Long Do You Want to Own the Business?

Are you leaving corporate America late in life and just trying to bridge the gap to retirement, or is entrepreneurship your actual retirement plan? Is this the beginning of your career or just the next chapter?

Many small business owners want to sell their business in order to fund their retirement. However, a recent survey found that while that's true for 78 percent of small business owners, fewer than 30 percent have actually crafted a succession plan.

As with any endeavor, it's important that you have an idea of when you'll be finishing. Certainly, that doesn't mean you must be out the door on that future date you're planning on, but this is the date you'll plan around. Otherwise, you risk selling the business at less than optimal value. For instance, if you want to own the franchise for only around five years, you don't want a franchise that historically matures to peak value in ten years.

What Will Happen When You're Ready to Sell?

Is this a business you want to rid yourself of completely? Do you envision keeping any equity? Do you already have a buyer in mind?

For many people, buying a franchise means the beginning of a family business that mom and dad plan to pass down to their children. However, if your children are still underage or just beginning their lives as adults, you definitely need a back-up plan. With more mature families with grown children who plan to work in the business, the parents should review their succession plan with the kids annually to make sure they still want to take over the business at some point.

Is the Franchise Recession-Resistant?

Just because you plan to sell your business in ten years doesn't mean the local economy is going to be optimal for you to sell at that time. If you can be flexible with your exit time, to ride out a slow turn in the economy, the state of the economy isn't a major consideration. However, experts estimate that roughly 4.5 million firms representing $10 trillion in assets will transition within the next decade and there is no way to know what the economy will look like in that time.

However, if you are committed to a specific time to sell your business, you probably want to make sure you're in a franchise that thrives whether the nation is in a period of recession or prosperity.

Does the Franchise Feature Recurring Revenue or Memberships?

Businesses that feature long-term contracts, subscriptions, or membership fees are generally very attractive when it comes time for you to sell your franchise because these financial frameworks offer a measure of income certainty and viability after you're gone.

The predictability that recurring revenue affords can give prospective buyers more confidence that they'll be able to succeed when they purchase your business. It gives them a better sense of how to plan for expenses, what their own growth strategy will look like and when they can plan for an exit strategy of their own.

How "Re-sellable" Is the Franchise?

This is an important question for the franchisor. You'll want to know how long franchisees generally own their franchises? What are the main reasons they decide to sell? How long are their franchises generally on the market, and what is their profit margin when they sell the business?

Established brands should be able to offer plenty of data on their units' salability. Moreover, you can look at the sector as a whole to see how well established units in that industry sell.

Does the Franchisor Offer Support for Selling?

The most important reason why people choose the franchising option is that it offers a proven model of success and, in many cases, unmatched support systems.

With that in mind, it's reasonable for you to ask the franchisor if it has a process in place to help franchise owners with their exit strategy. How involved is the corporate office in the sale? Does it offer marketing support to help you sell the business? Does it keep a database of candidates who have expressed interest in owning a franchise in your market?

Life as a small business owner has its rewards, but life *after* small business ownership should be equally rewarding. Planning for the latter at the beginning of your franchising endeavor will help ensure a smooth transition out of your business when the time is right.

FAMILY SUCCESSION PLANNING—HOW TO DO IT RIGHT

from Finance Your Business *by The Staff of Entrepreneur Media, Inc.*

While succession is challenging for all businesses, it often becomes even more complicated when family relationships must also be considered. This overlap between business and family creates many obstacles to the management, growth and sustainability of these companies. Blurred boundaries between ownership and management often lead to conflicts and jeopardize the companies' future.

While adopting sound governance practices can provide a valuable framework for family firms to address issues of sustainability and professionalism, they're usually not compulsory, as they are for large companies listed on the stock market. Family SMEs therefore rarely adopt corporate governance codes and principles, and even if they do, family emotions can influence strategic decision making, and especially succession.

Challenges in the Succession Process

Succession is a lengthy process that shouldn't be left to chance. Family businesses need to regard succession as an extended process of at least three years, with the roles and responsibilities of the predecessor and successor varying before, during and after the succession.

Before the succession takes place, the predecessor must mentor their chosen successor, closely nurturing their knowledge about all aspects of the business. During the succession process, the predecessor should begin to delegate increasing levels of responsibility, particularly decision-making power, to their successor. Finally, the predecessor will retire, leaving the business completely in the hands of the successor.

Learning to Let Go

Reluctance to let go is one of the most significant factors in the failure of succession in family businesses. Leaders are often unwilling to plan for succession due to an emotional attachment to the business, fear of retirement, loss of status, lack of power or even a lack of diversions outside work. This attachment to the business leads many family business leaders to maintain a leadership (or "consultant") position, even after retirement. While their experience can be invaluable, this continued presence can be perceived as a lack of trust in their successor, adversely affecting the decision-making process and confidence of employees and leading to frustration from the successor, as they live in the old leader's shadow.

Adopting a Culture of Trust

The willingness of a successor to take over is also crucially important in family business succession. Studies show the established leadership of family firms perceive commitment to the business as the most desired attribute in their future successor, ranking even higher than their competencies.

The generation gap and personality differences are the most common reasons for disagreements between the current leader and their chosen successor. To avoid this, family businesses must adopt a culture of trust and mutual respect, supported by open communication. This will allow for an effective transfer of knowledge and social capital and ensure the continuation of the business.

Avoiding Conflict

Nepotism and sibling rivalry are common in failed succession plans, underlining the importance of a shared vision among family members, helping to keep the family united once the established leader steps down. Avoiding conflict between family members requires clear distribution of shares, roles and authorities, as well as the decision to base compensation on experience and competency. Emphasizing family values, loyalty and traditions can also play an important role in achieving a harmonious atmosphere and shared vision in family firms, all of which supports a smooth succession.

Handing over a business to the next generation is a real challenge to family businesses. However, it can be achieved by families working on their internal relationships to foster trust, open communication and mutual understanding between family members. At the end, having strong, solid family ties can help facilitate a smooth intergenerational transfer of wealth and reduce conflicts within families.

Turning the Business Over to Next of Kin

Handing down a family business is a dream of many entrepreneurs who want to see the business they started thriving in the hands of the next generation. But statistics show that succession can be riddled with challenges.

Wendy Sage-Hayward, a senior consultant at the Vancouver-based Family Business Consulting Group, says although many families may want to pass down their business, the succession process is often not thought through carefully enough to make the succession successful. Here are some handy guidelines to increase your chances of success.

Avoid Holding the Reins Too Tightly

Founders have a tendency to hang on to control, not allowing their kids to have enough say or enough investment in the business. "The entrepreneur typically does have a fairly strong control-oriented personality," says Sage-Hayward. Entrepreneurial characteristics tend to be very independent, autocratic and particular. It can be difficult for entrepreneurs to let go of those tendencies, but Sage-Hayward says that's exactly what needs to happen in order to have a successful succession.

Eliminate Entitlement

Just because your last name is "Jones" doesn't mean you should automatically get a seat at the Jones Company's boardroom table, says Sage-Hayward. She recommends entrepreneurs set expectations around how kids will get to participate in the family business. Often, kids will be encouraged to go outside the company for work experience and education so they can bring those experiences back into the family business.

Build the Skill Sets of the Next Generation

One of the biggest mistakes Sage-Hayward says she's seen in family businesses is that the founders have been so busy working in and building the business that they haven't spent the time to work on building the skill set or engagement of the successive generation. "Working on the business means you're developing the next generation, engaging them, helping them get the kind of skills and capabilities that they need to take it over," says Sage-Hayward. Building stewardship in family members means holding regular family meetings to involve other family members in the key conversations so they understand the ins and outs of the business and are prepared to take it over when the time comes.

Gauge Their Interest

Sometimes founders have a dream that their children will take over the family business, but the children simply aren't interested. Sage-Hayward says this often happens when the founder shuts out the family from the day-to-day interactions of the business or is so busy building the business and not spending time with their families that the kids begin to resent the business and want nothing to do with it when they get older. Involving kids in the business at an early age in a positive way is the best way to ensure they'll be enticed to join the business later on. "Succession planning starts from a very early age," says Sage-Hayward, "building work ethic, building the understanding of the business and building the mindset."

Be Prepared to Let Go

Ruling from the grave is one of the worst mistakes entrepreneurs can make when handing a business down to the next generation. Trying to set up structures that will control what the next generation can do rather than allowing them to run the company will only cause leadership ambiguity and create a stressful work environment for those family members who are left to run the company. Founders should be emotionally and mentally prepared to walk away from the business completely when the time comes around.

ENTREPRENEUR VOICES SPOTLIGHT: INTERVIEW WITH KANIKA TOLVER

Kanika Tolver is no ordinary "social-preneur." This highly decorated information technology federal government professional, rebel entrepreneur, and Certified Professional Coach is a serial innovator who's fueled by an extraordinary commitment to social change and helping others create their own epic lives.

Tolver is the CEO and Founder of Career Rehab, LLC in Washington, DC. Career Rehab focuses on assisting career transformations for students, professionals, and retirees. Her company provides career coaching programs, events, webinars, and digital resources to help people reach their career goals. She has been featured on CNN, CBS Radio, Yahoo!, Glassdoor, Entrepreneur, *The Washington Post*, and in a variety of radio interviews. A self-professed "tech geek" and career technologist enamored by the latest and greatest gadgetry, Tolver is also an advocate for people of color who want to become more involved in science and technology. She is the author of *Career Rehab* (Entrepreneur Press, 2020).

Entrepreneur: How did you get into the world of rehabbing careers? What is your origin story?

Tolver: I started rehabbing careers ten years ago when I began writing and editing my family members and friends resumes. They would be looking for a job right out of college or a better paying job and once I rewrote their resume, they would always get the job. But, it wasn't until six years ago that I started rehabbing my own career and I saw a lot of success with landing mid-six-figure jobs at the age of 30. So, I started sharing my success stories on social media. Then, I created my career coaching practice Career Rehab, LLC to help people find career happiness.

Since I had suffered from career depression, I was better able to share my career development and career branding strategies that helped me land job interviews with Microsoft, Deloitte, Intel, and Booz Allen Hamilton. I began to look at myself as a product and help other professionals with their personal branding transformation for their career goals. Today, I have career coached hundreds of professionals and have spoken to thousands of professionals on how to brand, market, and sell themselves in their dream jobs. But before they could do this, they needed to rehab their careers for success.

Entrepreneur: What are some of the challenges for people who are unhappy with their current jobs who want to get "unstuck"? What advice would you give to overcome/address those challenges?

Tolver: The most popular challenges faced by professionals who are unhappy is career fear and career depression. Career fear blocks professionals from being able to map out their career blueprint. Some professionals I career coach have been working the same job for 20 years. They are now afraid of starting over with a career change or finding a new job. Even though they feel stuck, their current familiarity does not bring uncertainty despite lack of career growth or bad leadership. Career depression drains people emotionally, making professionals feel like there's no hope. Some professionals have given up on taking or asking for new training, earning advanced degrees or applying to new roles. Their personal life or work life becomes a huge stumbling block for career progression.

My advice to professionals struggling from career fear and depression is to check themselves into Career Rehab. It's time for them to assess their current career state and begin to map out their career roadmap. As they shift their mindset from a "cannot" attitude to a "can-do" attitude, it will become easier to map out their career goals and identify a solution for each goal. When we shift, our thinking, we can modify our behaviors. You career roadmap should identify your career, professional training, salary, and work-life balance goals. You have to map out how you want your life to be if you want career happiness.

Entrepreneur: What are some of the best ways people can rehab their careers beyond switching jobs? What do those options look like?

Tolver: Rehabbing your career is not all about finding a new job; for some it may be about promoting career growth within your current role. For instance, you can volunteer for more responsibility, apply for a detail role within your company, or shadow a senior-level employee who can teach you new professional skills. Also, you can self-study for professional certifications as well as read industry-related books and blogs on a daily basis. The key is to continue to grow your interpersonal, leadership, and technical skills. Career rehab is about restoring or building upon the career foundation you already have today.

As a professional, you can utilize online learning tools like LinkedIn Learning, Udemy, and YouTube to watch online videos that can help you further your industry knowledge or learn something new for a career change. You can also learn from your team members or network with other professionals in your organization who may be willing to mentor you as you develop new skills. I am huge fan of networking with professionals on LinkedIn because it's so important to connect with industry leaders, professionals, and authors who are subject-matter experts in your field. These professionals can share their knowledge with you and may help you land a new job. We, as professionals, have to continue to expand our professional network and knowledge if we don't want to become stuck.

Entrepreneur: How do you know it's the right time to officially make the break with your current career situation? How can people create an exit strategy?

Tolver: You, as a professional, will know when you have endured enough of feeling stuck and unhappy. As you rehab yourself—meaning you have worked on developing the foundation of your personal brand and professional knowledge—then it's time to market yourself to the world. I like to call this "market yourself like an ad" which means you are ready to use an updated resume, your LinkedIn profile, and job board profiles like Indeed to apply to new career roles that will bring you the career happiness you deserve.

You career strategy is the execution of your career roadmap. After you have earned a professional certification or gained more technical professional experience, it's time to develop a timeline to plan out when you would like to be in a new role. As you build your exit strategy, identify what type of work will make you happy and what type of company culture you are looking for. Your career exit strategy framework should be built and executed without career fear and depression. The exit strategy process will be accompanied by a sense of uncertainty, but you should welcome your new career rehab journey with open arms.

Entrepreneur: What are some ways you can rehab your career if you don't necessarily want to change companies? How can you get happier where you are?

Tolver: It's important to utilize your talents and gifts on the job. Professionals usually become happier or unstuck when they are working on projects they are passionate about at their current companies. When you hear of new projects or volunteer opportunities, ask your manager if you can participate and always express to them how you will add value. Another way you can rehab your career is to take advantage of their training budget, tuition reimbursement programs and detail opportunities. Also, try to network with other professionals by going to lunch with new people or grabbing a cup of coffee together where you can chat with each other about new career opportunities or just to have a casual professional chat.

One of the best ways to promote happiness where you are is to develop a healthy relationship with your manager and team members. I think we have all become unhappy on a job because we have or have had a bad relationship with the people we work with. When you enjoy what you do and who you do it with, life is so much easier. At times, you may not be able to fix your relationships with your co-workers or managers, but it's worth trying. I also advise you to develop a healthy relationship with yourself because this will allow you to better identify what pleases you within your career space. Lastly, you can become happier by incorporating a work-life balance, working from home and exercising daily. Career rehab requires hard work and patience. I know you can do it!

HOW YOU GET BACK INTO THE BUSINESS WORLD AFTER TAKING A BREAK

Debby Carreau

Whether you leave to raise a family, care for aging parents, go on medical leave, do your MBA or even travel, reentering the work world after an extended period of time can be tricky.

The most common reason people step out of the workforce, other than to retire, is to raise a family fulltime and disproportionately this responsibility falls to women. The statistics on women who chose to exit the workforce are staggering: Only

74 percent who take time out will return and only 40 percent of those will return full time.

This is always surprising considering 93 percent of women express an intention to return to the workforce, but shift their priorities. So how do you beat the odds and successfully transition back into the business world? Be strategic and plan your return. Treat your transition like a job. Haphazardly submitting your resume to 100 random online postings is not likely to land you a lasting fulfilling career.

Decide What You Want to Do

Ask yourself these questions:

- How much and where would you like to work? (FT, PT, freelance, downtown, from home, etc.)? When you are re-entering the workforce is a great time to reflect on what you really want to do.
- Have your interests changed? Many people find after a break or significant life change they are passionate about different things. I know many people who have moved from finance and law to more creative or flexible endeavors such as interior design and often this is an optimal time to start a business or buy a franchise.

- Many entrepreneurs say during time away from office it can be easier to identify a gap in the market and start a consumer business. Many great companies have been started this way.

- Do your research. There is great data available to see where the most promising career and wage growth is. Government labor websites will tell you everything you need to know about growing industries, job openings, and wage trajectories of specific roles in your region.

Get Rid of Self-Doubt

I believe the biggest thing holding people back when re-entering is lack of confidence and self-doubt. Think of yourself as coming back rejuvenated and refreshed—as an enhanced version of your former self. Remember over the course you your lifetime you have developed many skills, write yourself a list of your skills and accomplishments to revisit every time you start feeling insecure.

Identify and Update Your Skills

Even better than just identifying your skills is to stay current. When I talk to employers, they say the biggest skill barrier to successful re-entry is technology. Social media can really help here. Many of the programs employers use today closely mirror or even work off social media platforms. Also, a current web-friendly bio or resume and cover letter is important along with a current LinkedIn profile. Consider getting a professional to help with your resume, cover letter, and practice interviews.

Develop a Great Elevator Pitch

The more you practice it, the more confident you will become.

Start off with your strong headline, your value proposition and then spend the rest of the time backing up your position with evidence, case studies or testimonials. What do you do, or what role do you play? What result is achieved?

For example, an HR executive may say: "In my last role, I was the Executive Vice President of Human Resources for a large high growth multinational company with 30,000 employees. As a member of their executive team we worked to acquire new companies and successfully integrate their employees across the globe.

During my time in this role we acquired 10 companies and successfully transitioned 12,000 employees ensuring they were happy and settled in their new role. I am looking for a business opportunity where I can help make a difference in the work lives of employees. If you hear of a business or opportunity like this coming up I would really appreciate a referral."

Tell Others About Your Search

Accessing the hidden market is key because this is where the vast majority of jobs and opportunities are. Casually telling others that you're searching for employment or looking to acquire a business could make a difference and don't hesitate to use your social networks as much as your personal networks to get this message out.

If you know you are going to be stepping out of the workforce for a period of time what can you do proactively to ensure a smooth transition back to work? Try these tips:

1. Keep one foot in the door, stay connected with your co-workers and industry.
2. Consider doing something part time like volunteering, working a few hours a week, take on a small consulting assignment or even a home based business.
3. Stay active with on professional social media platforms like LinkedIn and Twitter by

following thought leaders, sharing relevant articles and engaging with your peers.

4. Keep reading industry publications or listening to podcasts. You would be really surprised how using current business language helps signal you are up to speed in your industry.

5. Perhaps most importantly don't feel pressure to do something during your time away from work. There is nothing wrong with taking a break and there is significantly less stigma around gaps in a resume today.

I still remember being on my smart phone in the delivery room when I had my son. At the time I thought it made me look like a dedicated employee; in hindsight that was silly. I am not sure what my coworkers were thinking but I can guarantee you it wasn't, "What a productive worker she is."

Don't Sweat Employment Gaps

Instead, you can do one of two things that work equally well. It depends on what you are more comfortable with. Right on your cover letter or in your discussions, explain you have taken time away for your specific reason and now are returning.

Or chronologically on your resume or LinkedIn profile fill the time away with part-time work, community involvement, or volunteer activities.

Stepping back into the game doesn't have to be overwhelming. Follow the data, understand what you are passionate about, and proactively search for the right opportunity.

HILARY DUFF ON WHY TAKING A BREAK CAN BE THE KEY TO YOUR CAREER

Danetha Doe

Hilary Duff, the beloved star from *Lizzie McGuire*, is now a mom and a total boss who calls the shots on all her collaboration deals. After her Disney days, the actor has boldly spread her entrepreneurial wings and expanded her brand to include a vast array of business opportunities.

One of her most recent collaborations is with GlassesUSA.com, an online retailer of prescription eyewear. When Duff first learned that the company was interested in working with her, she was excited for the challenge. She was yearning for a creative outlet, and designing a collection felt like the perfect fit. She also loved that the brand was open to giving her complete freedom to design a collection.

After a few conversations, Duff and GlassesUSA. com decided to create the Muse x Hilary Duff Eyewear Collection, beautifully designed eyewear that was both affordable and comfortable. Demonstrating her commitment to women's empowerment, Duff chose to name each pair in the collection after a powerful woman in history.

The collection's success led to the Bold Capsule, a limited-edition collection of Muse x Hilary Duff. Designing a collection with a well-known brand is a dream for many bloggers and creative business owners. So, we asked Duff about what advice she could share with other entrepreneurs on how to make this dream a reality.

Entrepreneur: How did the conversations begin with GlassesUSA.com? Did they approach you or vice-versa?

Duff: This was a totally unexpected partnership. I have regular conversations with my team about ideas I have and the direction I want to take my brand. I am approached a lot about various opportunities, and my team does an incredible job of vetting them.

With this, GlassesUSA.com reached out to do a one-off Instagram post wearing their glasses. I'm a total sunglass junkie and I loved their brand, so I said sure! After that post, the relationship organically grew into a collaboration where they asked me to design a capsule collection.

The one-off post was a great way to test the waters to see if we were a good fit for each other and if it felt authentic to me to explore a deeper partnership.

Entrepreneur: You exude such poise and have your "feet firmly on the ground" in your interviews. You've shared that checking in with yourself is very important in order to discover yourself. What does it mean, to you, to check in with yourself?

Duff: I'm still on the path of discovering myself. What has helped me is to write things down. Whether it's business, personal, or reflections on parenting, it helps me to discover what's really going on inside. From there, I lean into what feels good, even if it feels uncomfortable. Being uncomfortable leads to bold opportunities, and bold opportunities are where dreams come alive.

Entrepreneur: You've had an outstanding career with incredible longevity. What are one or two key business decisions you've made, that have enabled you to have a successful, long career?

Duff: You know, I got really lucky with *Lizzie McGuire*. I booked that opportunity at a really young age, and it established a great platform for me—and a chance to build a career based on authenticity, because I was so much like Lizzie. People loved her and, in turn, loved me. Since then, I've continued to be honest, relatable, and approachable. I'm an open book, and that has really helped me navigate business relationships, because I only do projects that are authentic to me. Because of that, I also take my time with decisions. I don't rush into anything that doesn't feel right.

The other decision I have made is to take breaks and reflect. I took a big break before and after my first pregnancy, and that space allowed me to reevaluate what was no longer working for me. I broke away from my team of ten years. After having someone else make all of my business decisions, do all of my negotiating, it was time for me to grow up and be an entrepreneur. I surrounded myself with new people and made more decisions for my business.

Entrepreneur: What are one or two business lessons you have learned with your GlassesUSA.com partnership?

Duff: You know when GlassesUSA.com approached me, I was very intimidated. Here's this big machine that wants to work with me, and I thought, What do I have to offer? But, then I checked in with myself and realized that I absolutely have something to offer. I have a lot of value to bring to the table.

I know what women around the age of 30 want to wear, how they feel, their dreams, desires, and goals. Not only am I one of those women, but a lot of my followers are those women and have grown up with me from my *Lizzie McGuire* days. That knowledge and expertise I have is valuable to a company seeking to connect with this group of women. That's the biggest lesson I've learned from this partnership. The importance of knowing your worth and sticking to it.

Entrepreneur: How do you feel your Muse x Hilary Duff collection and featuring women leaders/ pioneers fits into today's culture?

Duff: It is so important. I am inspired by women who have paved the way for us by doing something bold, something uncomfortable and have fought to make their dream a reality. Wearing something with their name on it gives me confidence to continue to pursue my dreams and I hope it does the same for others.

Entrepreneur: What is your recommendation to an up-and-coming blogger who wishes to create partnerships with brands? How do you balance the desire to grow your business with being authentic?

Duff: Well, if I am completely honest, I have to say that I'm a little envious of bloggers because they have created a space for themselves where their readers actively seek them out for their authenticity. With that said, my one piece of advice is to keep doing what you're doing and focus on knowing your worth. You and your work are valuable. Your message matters and brands are eager to work with you, just as you are.

PREPARING FOR A SMOOTH REENTRY INTO THE WORKFORCE

Sandy Mobley

For many women who take significant time off from their careers to raise a family, the prospect of reentering the workforce is daunting. They're concerned their skills are no longer sharp and that technology has thoroughly transformed the position they once knew so well. They see that their peers have moved ahead and fear they may have to start over.

And even if they're confident in their abilities and have kept their skills current, they worry that hiring managers won't give them a chance. But they shouldn't be.

For starters, they're part of a trend: More women are deciding to go back, and the rate has increased over recent years. According to an April 2018 report from the Bureau of Labor Statistics, the percentage of the population working or looking for work, for women with children under age 18, was 71.1 percent in 2017, up 0.6 percent from the previous year.

Second, there is help available, through community college programs and private programs like The Path Forward. Let's take a look at two case studies. See if you can see yourself in these women's stories.

Two Case Studies

I coached two women who had taken time off to raise their children. Kathy Newman* had been the VP of marketing for a financial services organization. Natalie Cummings* had been a regional manager for a national retail chain. Both had left those jobs to raise a family. Both had fallen behind in terms of technology trends in the workplace.

---

*Names have been changed to protect privacy.

That was certainly the predicament Kathy Newman faced. When she left her marketing job, social media and digital advertising had yet to dominate the marketing mix. But eight years later, when she wanted to return, Newman felt ill-prepared for the new marketing world.

To turn that around, she adopted a three-prong strategy: re-establish her professional network, obtain relevant training, and pursue contract work. Newman also met with past colleagues to learn how the industry had changed and what new skills were required. At professional association meetings, she learned about cutting-edge marketing campaigns and absorbed others' advice about moving into the digital space.

She realized that her core knowledge was still relevant but also recognized what she had yet to learn about social and digital marketing.

To do that, Newman attended conferences, read articles, took online tutorials, and attended classes on social media at a local university. She picked up the new skills quickly, but she needed to freshen her resume by adding more relevant work experience. With the gig economy in full swing, she took on freelance and part-time marketing jobs that strengthened her skills, created a track record of success and, most importantly, boosted her confidence.

Her strategy worked: After a year, Newman accepted a full-time position that matched her experience and skills.

Natalie Cummings, meanwhile, didn't have the luxury of taking a year to prepare to return to the workforce. Her husband had been laid off and she needed a job "yesterday." She had worked in retail as a manager before taking four years off to raise her twin boys. So she reached out to her former employer. The company, it turned out, was delighted to have her back—but as a salesperson, not a manager—and she was assured she'd move up rapidly once she proved herself.

Cummings, however, wasn't interested in starting over, and after a two-month job search secured an alternate position in management at another retail organization.

Accepting and Rejecting the "Penalty"

The financial pressure Cummings felt to find work quickly could have caused her to accept a lower-level position as a penalty for taking time off. But she was confident her skills were just as valuable as they had been four years ago.

If anything, Cumming's time with her young family had sharpened many foundational work skills, from emotional intelligence and mediation to problem analysis and multitasking. Her time off had also fostered her resolve to find work that was meaningful, not just a job. She reasoned that time away from loved ones must be time well spent.

Examine Your Feelings First

If, like Newman and Cummings, you want to reenter the workforce in a meaningful way, begin with an honest examination of your skills, passions, and work style:

- Review your past performance evaluations and ask people who know you well what they consider your greatest strengths. You will need to determine whether those skills are still in demand and what new skills you should acquire. If you are open to a new profession, a coach can offer assessment tools that match your skills to potential careers.

- Think, too, about your passions: Recognize the things that you love to do so much that you could do them all day without feeling bored or exhausted. If you want to apply your skills in an area you're passionate about, consider opportunities with organizations you admire and for causes that matter to you.

- Determine the type of environment you could thrive in. Do you like a collaborative culture or are you more productive working alone? Do you prefer a boss who is hands-on or one who is more supervisory? Think about what you appreciated about prior work environments and what you would have changed.

- Burnish your brand with a compelling resume and a profile posted on a professional social media site like LinkedIn. Many search firms use LinkedIn to source candidates, but it's also a good tool for reconnecting with former colleagues and finding people you know at companies where you might want to work. Set up informational interviews with those professionals to learn more about their company and industry.

All this assessment and preparation can serve to build your confidence. In their book *The Confidence Code*, Katty Kay and Claire Shipman noted that people who are confident are considered in a more positive light than those who are competent but lack confidence. When you believe in yourself, others will as well, paving the way for a smooth reentry into work that matters.

26

LAID-OFF CORPORATE WORKERS WHO BECAME FREE-THINKING ENTREPRENEURS

Jennifer Miller

In the fall of 2015, when Marty Mann's boss at General Electric called him into the office, he knew his days at the company were numbered. For seven years, Mann had been a welder at GE's locomotive plant in Erie, PA. Built just over a century ago, the 340-acre complex originally employed and housed thousands of workers and defined the city's economic and social life. But layoffs had become common, and 2015 saw a downsizing of

1,500 employees. Mann was one. "Yeah, I was mad," he says. "You used me and then got rid of me. But when it's time to go, it's time to go."

Mann has lived in Erie his entire life, and everyone here—his wife, kids, grandkids, and friends— knows him as a no-bullshit kind of guy. Middle-aged and meaty, he prefers oversize T-shirts and dirt-crusted work boots. His graying hair is rarely brushed, and his days are fueled by whole pots of sugar-saturated coffee, beer, and drugstore doughnuts. But he's a talented welder. So upon being shown the door at GE, he began looking for another job. Nobody in his field was hiring locally. A buddy told him about an opportunity in South Carolina, but Mann couldn't imagine leaving his family behind. "What are you going to do?" he says. "Work in McDonald's? Be a greeter at Walmart? At GE, I was making between $33 and $40 an hour, plus benefits."

Out of Necessity, a New Beginning

Mann started to struggle. His unemployment benefit was running out, he'd received no severance, and his utilities were about to be shut off. Then, one night at a bar, Mann's younger brother John, who had also been laid off from GE, suggested the two of them start a business fixing and outfitting motorcycles. Mann was a skilled mechanic and something of an artist when customizing bikes. But he was skeptical. The brothers had always worked for someone else. Neither had experience with small business. But Mann concluded he had no other option. "If you can't get a job," Mann says, "you've got to make a job."

In July 2016, the brothers opened Mann's Cycle Works. And in doing so, they became what economists call *necessity entrepreneurs*. It's a term used to describe people who start a business because they struggle to find employment. Nobody officially counts how many people fit the description, but experts say the group is growing—initially fueled by those who lost jobs during the recession and, today, by communities where once-dominant industries are fading.

Though necessity entrepreneurs may come from hardship, they're an important group to watch. These are the people creating solutions to their own problems. "Just because a business starts in a recession or out of necessity doesn't mean it won't be very good or successful," says Robert Fairlie, a professor of economics at the University of California, Santa Cruz. He found that while regular entrepreneurship goes down during economic downturns, necessity entrepreneurship goes up. And, he says, roughly half of all Fortune 500 companies were started during economic recessions.

That's why, for an entrepreneur of any background, it can be helpful to see how a necessity entrepreneur succeeds. Starting a business from scratch is inherently risky, but it's even more so when you lack resources, a financial safety net, and business experience. Yet necessity entrepreneurs do it—adjusting not just to the realities of business but to a new self-identity, all while under intense financial pressure. Mann has the scars to show it. His entrepreneurship nearly ruined him. His savings evaporated, his relationships were strained, and he nearly closed up shop. But he didn't quit. Instead, he turned necessity into opportunity. He drew upon his expertise, his creativity and his fortitude in ways he never thought possible. Like most entrepreneurs— whether driven by necessity or opportunity—he learned to reinvent himself.

Unlocking the Entrepreneur Identity

Consider your relationship with the word entrepreneur. Perhaps you see it as a goal or a calling, or maybe even an identity. But to understand a guy like Mann, set that all aside. He never considered himself an entrepreneur. He didn't know anyone who did.

"Entrepreneurship means something bigger, sexier, techier than they would consider themselves," says Lisa Hutson, director of Lorain County Community College's Small Business Development Center, in Ohio. She learned this last year, after receiving a grant to promote entrepreneurship across her Rust Belt region. Visits to union halls, urban league centers, and El Centro offices all flopped; she was met with skepticism or outright disinterest. When she offered an "Introduction to Entrepreneurship" class, almost nobody came.

It was a puzzle to her. Locals were entrepreneurial; they were talented and skilled, and many had side hustles. But as she came to understand, they didn't see themselves as entrepreneurs. "Steve Jobs is an entrepreneur, not the beauty salon owner," she says, explaining their mindset. Also, they weren't acculturated to thinking of themselves as potential bosses and owners. For so long, a corporate machine provided stability in their community— which meant individual success came by fitting into a system. Among the professional elite, " 'disruption' means founding a successful startup," writes law professor Joan Williams in her book *White Working Class: Overcoming Class Cluelessness in America*. "Disruption, in working-class jobs, just gets you fired."

Harnessing the Power of Hustle

In Lorain, Hutson realized she needed to talk differently. She dropped the word entrepreneurship and began evangelizing "hustle." Getting laid off from one factory and starting over in the next—that required hustle. Managing a household budget when one or both parents were out of work—that required hustle. And of course, running a side gig—be it selling crafts on Etsy or brewing homemade beer to sell at the local farmers' market—was the result of hustle.

This reframing helped, but it wasn't enough. Hutson also had to convince people that hustle was the same as creativity and innovation (and disruption!), even if it didn't produce the next iPhone.

Jamie Smith remembers struggling with that transition. He grew up in West Virginia coal country, surrounded by people who thought coal was all they could do. He worked in coal as well, but he studied marketing and coding at night, anticipating that one day he'd be laid off—and in 2010, he was. Still, he says, the idea of starting his own business seemed impossible. "It was shocking and scary," he says. If it hadn't been for the encouragement of his friend Jason Lockart, a graphic designer from New Jersey, who had not grown up in a one industry town, Smith says he might never have taken the leap. In 2012, the friends founded Kid in the Background. Today they have a staff of four and work with national organizations like Boy Scouts of America. Still, Smith feels like an impostor at times—as though this can't be a real career. "I still second-guess myself," he says.

As Mann set up his motorcycle shop, he faced these same cultural challenges. Nearly everyone in his family had been a GE employee. His great-aunt was one of its first local hires. His uncles did assembly work there. His mother wound coil and assembled circuit boards there until she died at 58. Mann himself dropped out of high school at 16, knowing he'd be able to find similar work. He spent 23 years as a welder at Ridg-U-Rak before moving to GE, where he worked on large trucks and locomotive fans. "It used to be nothing to walk out one [factory] door, go down the street and into another door and say, 'Do you need a welder?'" he says. "We've been working at large companies for decades and decades."

Now Mann had no choice but to try something new.

In big cities, first-time business owners have a fundamental advantage that they may not appreciate: They're surrounded by examples of success. Entrepreneurship is visible there. That's not always the case in working-class communities. "Everybody they know is in that blue-collar world," says Hutson. "Without those mentors, they just can't see themselves doing it."

Community-based organizations are starting to fill that gap, says Hutson—from SBDC offices and other agencies that offer free Skype consultations, to inexpensive business classes at community colleges, to local economic development offices that help new entrepreneurs find funding. Hutson often adopts the role of cheerleader for clients who have bad or no credit and haven't really considered their financials. "I constantly reinforce that they know more than they think," she says. "Getting organized and putting your thoughts on paper builds certainty."

Maximizing Connections, Overcoming Challenges

Mann would have benefited from a coach like Hutson, but that impostor syndrome kept him from seeking professional assistance. At the start, he was almost stubbornly resigned to his situation. Nobody's going to help someone like me, he thought. I have to do it on my own.

But Mann did have another kind of support—one that is absolutely an advantage of tight-knit, small towns: He knew a guy. Actually, he knew a few.

The first one helped out on real estate. Mann wasn't a candidate for a small-business loan, and he couldn't convince a landlord to rent him a space while he was on unemployment. But his friend Ron owned a defunct car wash down the street from GE. The place was a disaster. "You've never seen so many hypodermic needles," Mann says. "There was rebar in the parking lot, no doors, no heat. They were bringing hookers into car bays." Ron was happy to sell Mann the property, if only to see it cleaned up. And being sensitive to Mann's finances, he set up the world's most lax payment plan. "I pay when I can," Mann says.

Then Mann hit another snag. The neighbors didn't want him there. They worried his presence would attract even more unsavory types and filed a petition against him. So to prove his good intentions, Mann called in more friends. One buddy owned a blacktop company and helped Mann repave the parking lot at a steep discount. Another buddy owned a garage door company and installed soundproof doors. Mann also installed cameras on the garage to guard against illegal activity and built a bench at the edge of the property, where local kids could wait for their school bus. When he won 16 hams in a raffle, he donated them to families on his block. The neighbors were appeased.

Building Community

In 2016, after less than a year of existence, Mann's Cycle Works won the Commitment to Erie Award for new business. But he almost didn't attend the ceremony. The idea of entrepreneurship —of the power of entrepreneurship—still hadn't sunk in. "It's just a bike shop," he said at the time. "What's the big deal?"

But actions like his radiate far beyond one store or neighborhood. Mann's new shop had created a little business hub for bike enthusiasts. His friends soon opened a biker bar across the street, which then increased traffic at the convenience store and tattoo parlor on the same block. "As more people become aware of how small businesses invest in the community and [improve] the health of the environment," says Maggie Horne, director of Gannon University's Small Business Development Center in Erie, "they're more willing to value what these businesses bring to the table."

Which is to say that here in Erie, one of the fastest-shrinking cities in America, where laid-off workers may be reluctant to open new businesses, Mann was starting to provide the kind of story that entrepreneurs in big cities see all the time: He was showing what's possible.

On a warm afternoon, Mann stands by the open door of his garage, drinking strong coffee and shooting the breeze. His friend Tom sits in a folding chair squeezed in between half a dozen or more bikes, all in various stages of disrepair. "I've got to get these bikes out of here," Mann says. "Otherwise I can't get new ones in." But he doesn't expect that to happen soon. Many of their owners owe him money for parts. Until they pay up, he's stuck.

"He's got a community, you know?" says Tom, turning to me. "When they say they'll pay, he tries to take their word for it." Tom shakes his head like he both admires Mann and worries about him.

This community, largely a crew of middle-aged locals, was of course vital to helping launch Mann's business. But it's since become something of a liability. People hire Mann, unsure of when or if they can pay him. They've come in so often to ask repair questions—treating him like a living YouTube instructional video—that he hung a sign that says $75 shop minimum. Then he'll reinforce it. "Questions are free, answers $75," he tells people. But still, Mann can't always draw a hard line. When a friend needed $6,000 to pay for his mother's funeral, Mann declined to charge him for an extensive job. He did the same when this friend's wife needed emergency surgery.

Learning Hard Lessons about Trust

Mann knows most customers will try to make it up to him. But not everyone will. It's something he learned the hard way—most difficultly, he says, from his brother John, the one who encouraged him to open the shop in the first place.

At the outset, John said he'd handle all their company's finances, and Mann agreed. Had they talked to experts, they'd have been advised against this. "In the beginning, people don't want to talk about what happens if it derails or goes badly," says Hutson. She always recommends that clients hire an accountant to manage finances and an attorney to draft a formal partnership agreement, even among family. But the Mann brothers didn't.

In Mann's telling, the relationship quickly devolved. John would come in late and then just sit at the garage desk, smoking and chatting up neighborhood characters. Then, in September 2016, they got into a big blowup at the shop about a contractor John had hired. "He started yelling at me," Mann says. "And I said, 'Why don't you just shut the fuck up or get the fuck out?'"

So John did. A month went by with no sight of him. Truth be told, Mann was relieved. But one day, Mann tried to order some motorcycle parts and his debit card was declined. With a sinking feeling, he drove over to the bank. His account should have had about $20,000 in it, but it was empty. Mann says John took it all. Later, he says, he learned that John also hadn't paid the business's taxes—and the IRS was calling. (John couldn't be reached for comment, but two of Mann's friends, who knew John and have been frequent visitors of the shop, as well as Mann's daughter, confirmed Mann's version of the story.)

"I didn't think I was going to make it, to be honest," Mann says. "It was devastating." To survive, he expanded his business to start fixing snow blowers, which is useful during Erie's heavy winters, and scored a $1,500 job from his mailman, which helped pay off some debt. He's still digging out, but now he believes it's possible.

This was Mann's learning moment. He resolved to stop leaning on family and friends so he could stand on his own. He hired an accountant to get the books in order. He's working harder to buy his building outright. "This year," Mann says, his shop still full of unpaid work, "I'm starting over."

All Roads Lead to Main Street

Over the past two years, as Mann has become more comfortable with owning a business, something intangible but important has shifted: The man who never called himself an entrepreneur has started to talk and even feel like one.

"People need to wake up and see that the big businesses are dying," Mann says. "The small shops, those are growing." His friends now come asking his advice, inspired to follow his lead. In addition to the bar across the street, Mann's friends have started a construction company, a landscaping business, an auto body garage and a concrete-laying company. And Mann, meanwhile, is starting to think bigger. He wants to open a retail space in Erie and expand Mann's Cycle Works to warm climates—South Carolina and Florida—where there's good winter business. His daughter wants to quit her receptionist job and work with him, and as soon as he's making enough money, he says, he'll welcome it.

The change is happening more broadly, too, according to people who work for small-business organizations. They credit entrepreneurship being in the American zeitgeist; it's filtering into all corners. "Even 10 years ago, people didn't tell their stories of entrepreneurship as much as they do now," Hutson says. Kenneth Louie, director of the Economic Research Institute of Erie, says he's seen many locals start a new business and transform as a result. "It takes a lot in terms of attitudes and motivations and assets," he says.

There's an old line entrepreneurs say about themselves: If we could do anything else, we would. That's meant as a testament to passion. Entrepreneurship is so difficult, and can be so thankless, that the only people who do it are those who cannot imagine feeling fulfilled any other way. Mann, of course, came to it through a different kind of necessity—less passion and more economics. "I'm still here" is about the best compliment he'll give himself when you ask how business is going. He jokes that Ringo Starr's "It Don't Come Easy" is his theme song. But like anyone who sets out on their own, he's now devoted to the road ahead. He appreciates its balance of risk and reward. That's entrepreneurship. "I keep going," Mann says. "I just keep going."

PART IV
EXIT STRATEGIES AND KICKASS COMEBACKS—REFLECTIONS

Everyone needs an exit strategy. Whether you are a lifelong intrapreneur preparing to leave the corporate world for the happy trails of retirement or a side hustler ready to make the big leap into the entrepreneurial unknown, you need to have a plan. And to do that, you need to know where the exits are.

So, you prepare. You make lists, build contacts, create contingency plans for the teams you will leave behind, and—most importantly—you get your own financial house in order. It's a lot to do, but the important thing to remember is that building a strong exit strategy is not a task best saved for last. Your exit strategy should be a part of your work life from day one. That's not to say that you should always operate with one foot out the corporate door, but rather that you should have an idea of where you'd like to head in your career and a plan for making it happen.

In the same vein, you also need to have a plan in place for the day your new venture goes south. Hopefully, it will never happen and you won't have to scramble to pick up the pieces, but having funds and contingency plans in place will help cushion the blow if you have to close up shop or reinvent your business.

Whether that last day arrives on a schedule you set or it appears suddenly and you find yourself packing your desk up sooner than you'd planned, you'll be ready. And you'll leave on your own terms, fully prepared for what comes next, whatever that may be.

RESOURCES

(In Order of Appearance)

Thank you to our talented Entrepreneur contributors whose content is featured in this book. For more information about these contributors, including author bios, visit us at www.entrepreneur.com.

1. Isa Watson, "Not Your Parents' Career Development," *Entrepreneur*, September 20, 2018, www.entrepreneur.com/article/319624.

2. Sharon E. Jones, "3 Unwritten Rules of the Corporate World That Women Need to Know," *Entrepreneur*, November 6, 2018, www. entrepreneur.com/article/322014.

3. Angela Kambouris, "Drive Real Innovation by Re-discovering Your Intrinsic Entrepreneurial Mindset," *Entrepreneur*, October 2, 2018, www. entrepreneur.com/article/319808.

4. Suresh Sambandam, "How I Became the CEO of a Multimillion-Dollar Company—Without Going to College," *Entrepreneur*, March 19, 2018, www.entrepreneur.com/article/310550.

5. Elizabeth Closmore, "I Went From Entry-Level to Leader in My Field in Just 10 Years. Here's How I Did It." *Entrepreneur*, November 16, 2017, www.entrepreneur.com/article/304042.

6. Michelle Burrell, "3 Tips for Advancing Your Career as a Woman," *Entrepreneur*, July 24, 2018, www.entrepreneur.com/article/317225.

7. Murray Newlands, "10 Side Hustles Ideal for Making Some Spare Cash In the Evenings," *Entrepreneur*, September 20, 2017, www. entrepreneur.com/article/300449.

8. Jeff Bonaldi, "Why You Should Start a Business Only While You Have a Job," *Entrepreneur*,

December 17, 2018, www.entrepreneur.com/article/324255.

9. William Harris, "Career-Minded Millennials Should Think Twice Before Starting a Side Hustle," *Entrepreneur*, June 21, 2018, www.entrepreneur.com/article/314518.

10. Erica Liu Williams, "5 Ways to Kickstart Your Side Hustle While Leveraging Your 9-to-5," *Entrepreneur*, December 18, 2018, www.entrepreneur.com/article/324269.

11. Raj Jana, "I Built My Multimillion-Dollar Side-Hustle While Working a Full-Time Job and So Can You," *Entrepreneur*, October 12, 2018, www.entrepreneur.com/article/320976.

12. Syed Balkhi, "4 Tips to Take your Side Hustle to the Next Level," *Entrepreneur*, August 7, 2018, www.entrepreneur.com/article/317726.

13. Mira Kaddoura, "Why Leaving Your Job Could Be the Smartest Career Move You'll Ever Make," *Entrepreneur*, November 2, 2018, www.entrepreneur.com/article/321265.

14. Carlos Gil, "How to Transition From a Corporate Job to Being an Entrepreneur," *Entrepreneur*, November 26, 2018, www.entrepreneur.com/article/323645.

15. Megha Hamal, "The 5 Most Important Questions to Consider Before Beginning Your Entrepreneurial Journey," *Entrepreneur*, September 6, 2018, www.entrepreneur.com/article/319284.

16. Solange Lopes, "How to Transition From the Corporate World to Entrepreneurship as a Working Woman," *Entrepreneur*, June 5, 2018, www.entrepreneur.com/article/312191.

17. Nicolette Amarillas, "How to Turn Your Side Hustle Into a Full-Time Gig," *Entrepreneur*, July 10, 2018, www.entrepreneur.com/article/315497.

18. Dave Peck, "10 Things You Must Do Before Quitting Your Job to Start Your Company," *Entrepreneur*, June 18, 2017, www.entrepreneur.com/article/294251.

19. Candace Sjogren, "The Entrepreneurial Exit Strategy—Prepare Yourself," *Entrepreneur*, September 4, 2017, www.entrepreneur.com/article/299557.

20. The Staff of Entrepreneur Media, Inc., "How to Transition to Employee Ownership," *Entrepreneur*, July 12, 2017, www.entrepreneur.com/article/293893.

21. Jim Judy, "Before You Enter into Franchising, Consider Your Exit," *Entrepreneur*, January 18, 2018, www.entrepreneur.com/article/305076.

22. The Staff of Entrepreneur Media, Inc., "Family Succession Planning: How to Do It Right," *Entrepreneur*, July 5, 2017, www.entrepreneur. com/article/293892.

23. Debby Carreau, "Here's How You Get Back Into the Business World After Taking A Break," *Entrepreneur*, September 1, 2017, www. entrepreneur.com/article/297426.

24. Danetha Doe, "Hilary Duff Explains Why Taking a Break Can Be the Key to Your Career," *Entrepreneur*, September 21, 2018, www. entrepreneur.com/article/319579.

25. Sandy Mobley, "After the Exit Ramp: Preparing for a Smooth Reentry Into the Workforce," *Entrepreneur*, January 21, 2019, www. entrepreneur.com/article/326602.

26. Jennifer Miller, "How Laid-Off Corporate Workers Are Becoming Free-Thinking Entrepreneurs," *Entrepreneur*, August 8, 2018, www.entrepreneur.com/article/315157.

Reader's Notes